Zulu
phrasebook

First published 2008
Copyright © HarperCollins Publishers
Reprint 10 9 8 7 6 5 4 3 2 1 0
Typeset by Davidson Pre-Press, Glasgow
Printed in Malaysia by Imago

www.collinslanguage.com

ISBN 13 978-0-00-726686-9

Using your phrasebook

Your *Collins Gem Phrasebook* is designed to help you locate the exact phrase you need, when you need it, whether on holiday or for business. If you want to adapt the phrases, you can easily see where to substitute your own words using the dictionary section, and the clear, full-colour layout gives you direct access to the different topics.

The Gem Phrasebook includes:

- Over 70 topics arranged thematically. Each phrase is accompanied by a simple pronunciation guide which eliminates any problems pronouncing foreign words.

- A Top ten tips section to safeguard against any cultural faux pas, giving essential dos and don'ts for situations involving local customs or etiquette.

- Practical hints to make your stay trouble free, showing you where to go and what to do when dealing with everyday matters such as travel or hotels and offering valuable tourist information.

- Face to face sections so that you understand what is being said to you. These example mini-dialogues give you a good idea of what to expect from a real conversation.

- Common announcements and messages you may hear, ensuring that you never miss the important information you need to know when out and about.

- A clearly laid-out dictionary means you will never be stuck for words.

- A basic grammar section which will enable you to build on your phrases. *An asterisk is used throughout the book to refer you to the grammar section for further information.

It's worth spending time before you embark on your travels just looking through the topics to see what is covered and becoming familiar with what might be said to you.

Whatever the situation, your *Gem Phrasebook* is sure to help!

Contents

Using your phrasebook	3	Staying somewhere	48
		Hotel (booking)	48
Pronouncing Zulu	7	Hotel desk	51
		Camping	52
Top ten tips	13	Self-catering	53
Talking to people	15	Shopping	54
Hello/goodbye, yes/no	15	Shopping phrases	54
Key phrases	18	Shops	56
Polite expressions	21	Handicrafts and art	58
Celebrations	22	Food (general)	59
Making friends	22	Food (fruit and veg)	60
Work	25	Clothes	62
Weather	25	Clothes (articles)	63
		Maps and guides	65
Getting around	27	Post office	66
Asking the way	27	Photos	67
Bus and coach	29		
Train	31	Leisure	68
Taxi	35	Sightseeing and	
Boat and ferry	36	tourist office	68
Air travel	38	Entertainment	69
Customs control	40	Leisure/interests	70
		Safari/game reserves	70
Driving	41	Music	72
Car hire	41	Cinema	73
Driving	43	Theatre/opera	74
Petrol	43	Television	75
Breakdown	44	Sport	76
Car parts	45	Walking	77

Communications	79
Telephone and mobile	79
Text messaging	82
E-mail	82
Internet	84
Fax	85
Practicalities	86
Money	86
Paying	87
Luggage	88
Repairs	89
Laundry	90
Complaints	90
Problems	91
Emergencies	92
Health	96
Pharmacy	96
Doctor	97
Dentist	99
Different types of travellers	101
Disabled travellers	101
With kids	102
Business	103

Reference	106
Alphabet	106
Measurements and quantities	106
Numbers	108
Days and months	111
Time	114
Time phrases	115
Eating out	116
In a coffee shop	116
In a restaurant	118
Vegetarian	120
Traditional dishes	121
Wines	122
Spirits and liqueurs	124
Grammar	125
Culture and customs	135
Old names and new names	136
Zulu place names	137
Dictionary	138
English–Zulu	138
Zulu–English	214

Pronouncing Zulu

Zulu is a beautiful language, but will probably sound unlike any language you have ever heard before due to the presence of the so-called clicks. Like a number of other African languages, Zulu is also a tonal language. This implies the existence of vowel sounds that lend different meanings to words of the same spelling, e.g.: **'ubungane'** can mean 'childhood' or 'friendship'. Whole sentences may have double meanings depending on the tone that words are articulated with. The best way to master the correct tone and pronunciation is to listen carefully to Zulus when they speak.

The following pronunciation guide provides a description of mainly those Zulu speech sounds that are different from English sounds. The symbols for the clicks and the other sounds that don't exist in English are introduced. These symbols will be used wherever these sounds occur in words, phrases or sentences in the phrasebook.

You will notice that many of the Zulu words below are preceded by a hyphen. This is an indication that these words normally do not appear alone and are given a prefix when used in a conversation. For more information, see the Grammar section.

Vowels

Zulu vowels	Example	Sounds like	Symbol
a	-vala to close	'a' in English **arm** but more 'open'	aa
e	ibhubesi lion	'e' in English **bed**	e
	-letha to bring	'a' in English **mat**	e
i	-biza to call	'ee' in English **feed**	ee
o	-khombisa to show	'aw' in English **law**	o
	-thola to get	'o' in English **not**	o
u	-funa to want	'oo' in English **mood** but 'deeper'	oo

Consonants

Zulu consonants	Example	Sounds like	Symbol
b (without 'h')	-bona to see	'b' in English **bed** but 'softer'	b
bh	-bhala to write	'b' in English **bed**	b
k (between vowels)	ukudla food	'g' in English **gun**	g
k	inkinga problem	'c' in English **crowd** but without 'air'	k
kh	-khala to cry	'c' in English **cough**	k

Zulu consonants	Example	Sounds like	Symbol
ng	-ngena to enter	'ng' in English sing or with more pronounced 'g'	ng
p (without 'h')	-penda to paint	'p' in English paper but without 'air'	p
ph	phakathi inside	'p' in English paper	p
r	irandi rand	'r' in English red but 'rolled' more	r
t (without 'h')	itafula table	't' in English table but without 'air'	t
th	-thatha to take	't' in English table	t
tsh	-tshela to tell	'ch' in English chin but without 'air'	ch

Clicks and others

Zulu clicks etc.	Example	Explanation	Symbol
c	-cula to sing	place tip of tongue against back of top front teeth - pull tongue down sharply to create non-forced 'sucking' sound	/ʔ

Zulu clicks etc.	Example	Explanation	Symbol
ch	<u>ch</u>a no	pronounce like 'c' but add 'air'	/h
nc	-<u>nc</u>eda to help	'n' precedes 'c'	ŋ/
gc	-<u>gc</u>walisa to fill up	like 'c' but simultaneously add 'g'	/ġ
ngc	-<u>ngc</u>olile be dirty	like 'c' but simultaneously add 'ng'	ŋ/g
q	-<u>q</u>ala to start	articulated in middle of mouth - curl tongue backwards and place front part against middle of roof of mouth - pull down tongue quickly to produce 'clicking' sound	!?
qh	-<u>qh</u>otha to stoop	pronounce like 'q' but add 'air'	!h
nq	-<u>nq</u>oba to over- come	'n' precedes 'q'	ŋ!
gq	ngoM<u>gq</u>i- belo on Saturday	like 'q' but simultaneously add 'g'	!ġ
ngq	-<u>ngq</u>o- ngqoza to knock	like 'q' but simultaneously add 'ng'	ŋ!g

Zulu clicks etc.	Example	Explanation	Symbol
x	-<u>x</u>osha to chase away	articulated at back of mouth - keep tongue still against roof of mouth and suck in air through sides of mouth to produce 'clicking' sound	//ˀ
xh	i<u>xh</u>egu old man	pronounce like 'x' but add 'air'	//h
nx	<u>nx</u>ese sorry	'n' precedes 'x'	ŋ//
gx	-<u>gx</u>uma to jump	like 'x' but simultaneously add 'g'	//ġ
ngx	i<u>ngx</u>oxo discussion	like 'x' but simultaneously add 'ng'	ŋ//g
dl	-<u>dl</u>ala to play	place front part of tongue against roof of mouth behind front teeth - press out air at sides of mouth simultaneously producing 'voice' in throat - almost a combination of English 'd' and 'l'	ɮ
hl	-<u>hl</u>amba to wash	place front part of tongue against roof of mouth behind front teeth and then press out air at sides of mouth	ɬ

The second to last syllable in Zulu words is normally lengthened. This means that you should slightly lengthen '**-do-**' in the word '**Amadoda**' 'Men'. This lengthening is usually more pronounced in the last word of a sentence. In this phrasebook, length is indicated in the pronunciation line by means of a colon (:).

When numerals are used in Zulu, you can also pronounce them as you would in English, e.g. in the sentence '**Ngizovuka ngo-7**' 'I will wake at 7', you will actually use the word 'seven' in your Zulu sentence.

Top ten tips

1 Your attempts at speaking Zulu will most probably elicit an overwhelmingly positive reaction and a willingness to help you learn the language.

2 South Africans readily greet one another verbally. The person of higher standing will normally initiate the greeting.

3 Handshakes are another common form of greeting. The 'African Handshake', which is a variation of the conventional handshake, is also used in South Africa. You shake hands and without letting go, slip your hand around the other person's thumb. You then go back to the traditional handshake.

4 Traditionally in Zulu culture, excessive eye contact was avoided. In some areas, you may still find some women behaving this way when talking to men. This is a sign of respect.

5 Traditionally, a Zulu speaker will pass something to you using his right hand only, with the palm of the left hand supporting the right forearm. This is done to show you that you have nothing to fear and that nothing is being hidden away.

6 In rural areas of South Africa you may still find people wearing their traditional dress from time to time.

7 Zulus enjoy dancing and laughing, and you will often also hear people singing or whistling while they are going about their daily tasks.

8 Smoking in South Africa is prohibited in public buildings and on public transport. Special smoking sections are provided in restaurants.

9 It is customary to tip waiters, petrol pump attendants, tour guides, game rangers, porters and parking attendants. A 10% tip is generally given to waiters, while R2 - R5 is a guideline for petrol pump and parking attendants.

10 In South Africa driving under the influence of alcohol is a serious offence.

Talking to people

Hello/goodbye, yes/no

In Zulu, you need to differentiate between greeting one person and more than one person. If you want to show respect, you always greet people using the plural form. The same phrase is used in Zulu to say 'good morning', 'good afternoon' and 'good evening'. When saying goodbye, the person staying behind says 'go well', while the person leaving says 'stay behind well'.

There is no separate word for 'please' in Zulu – it is always part of a longer phrase. If you are asking for something say '**Ngi**cela' followed by what you are asking for, e.g. '**Ngi**cela ikhofi' for 'Please may I have some coffee'. If there is more than one person asking for something, say '**Si**cela ikhofi' 'Please may we have some coffee'. If you are asking another person to do something, say '**Ngi**cela **u**...' followed by the action word or verb that has to end on '**-e**', e.g. '**Ngi**cela **u**phinde' for 'Please repeat.' If you are asking more than one person to do something, say '**Ngi**cela **ni**...' followed by the action word or verb that has to end on '**-e**', e.g. '**Ngi**cela **ni**ngene' for 'Please come in.'

15

Please	**Ngicela...**
	ngee/ʔe:laa...
Thanks	**Ngiyabonga (kakhulu)**
(very much)	ngeeyaabo:ngaa (kaakoo:loo)
You're welcome!	**Nami ngiyabonga!**
	naa:mee ngeeyaabo:ngaa!
Yes	**Yebo**
	ye:bo
No	**Cha**
	/haa
Yes, please	**Ngingajabula**
	ngeengaajaaboo:laa
No, thanks	**Cha, ngiyabonga**
	/haa, ngeeyaabo:ngaa
OK!	**Kulungile!**
	kooloongee:le!
Sir/Mr	**Mnumzane**
	mnoomzaa:ne
Madam/Mrs/Ms	**Nkosikazi**
	nkoseegaa:zee
Miss	**Nkosazana**
	nkosaazaa:naa
Hello/Hi	**Sawubona**
	saawoobo:naa
(greeting more than one person)	**San'bonani**
	saanbonaa:nee
Goodbye/Bye (to one person leaving)	**Hamba kahle**
	haa:mbaa kaa:ɬe
(to more than one person leaving)	**Nihambe kahle**
	neehaa:mbe kaa:ɬe

(to one person staying)	**Sala kahle** saa:laa kaa:ɬe	
(to more than one person staying)	**Nisale kahle** neesaa:le kaa:ɬe	
Bye for now	**Sizobonana** seezobonaa:naa	
Good evening	**Sawubona** saawoobo:naa	
(to more than one person)	**San'bonani** saanbonaa:nee	
Goodnight	**Lala kahle** laa:laa kaa:ɬe	
(to more than one person)	**Nilale kahle** neelaa:le kaa:ɬe	
See you tomorrow	**Sizobonana kusasa** seezobonaa:naa koosaa:saa	
Excuse me! (to catch attention)	**Uxolo!** oo//ʔo:lo!	
Sorry!	**Nxese!** ŋ//e:se!	
I'm sorry	**Ngiyaxolisa** ngeeyaa//ʔolee:saa	
How are you?	**Unjani? or Usaphila?** oonjaa:nee? or oosaapee:laa?	
(to more than one person)	**Ninjani? or Nisaphila?** neenjaa:nee? or neesaapee:laa?	
Fine, thanks	**Ngikhona or Ngisaphila** ngeeko:naa or ngeesaapee:laa	
(to more than one person)	**Sikhona or Sisaphila** seeko:naa or seesaapee:laa	

And you?	**Wena unjani?** or **Wena usaphila?**
	we:naa oonjaa:nee? or we:naa
	oosaapee:laa?
(to more than	**Nina ninjani?** or **Nina nisaphila?**
one person)	nee:naa neenjaa:nee? or
	nee:naa neesaapee:laa?
I don't	**Angiqondi**
understand	angee!ʔo:ndee
I speak very little	**Ngisazi kancane kakhulu**
Zulu	**isiZulu**
	ngeesaa:zee kaaŋ/aa:ne
	kakoo:loo eeseezoo:loo

Key phrases
• •

When someone says something that you don't
understand, you can say '**Ngicela uphinde**' (ngee-
/ʔe:laa oopee:nde), which means 'Please repeat'.

the	*
the station	**isiteshi**
	eeste:shee
the shops	**izitolo**
	eezeeto:lo
a/one	*
a ticket	**ithikithi**
	eeteegee:tee
one stamp	**isitembu esisodwa**
(postage)	eestemboo eseeso:dwaa
a room	**ikamelo**
	eekaame:lo

18

one bottle	**ibhodlela elilodwa**
	eebo⁺e:laa eleelo:dwaa
some	*
some milk	**ubisi**
	oobee:see
Do you have...?	**Una...?***
(asking one person)	oonaa...?
(asking more than one person)	**Nina...?***
	neenaa...?
Do you have a room?	**Unalo ikamelo?**
	oonaa:lo eekaame:lo?
(asking more than one person)	**Ninalo ikamelo?**
	neenaa:lo eekaame:lo?
Do you have some milk?	**Unalo ubisi?**
	oonaa:lo oobee:see?
(asking more than one person)	**Ninalo ubisi?**
	neenaa:lo oobee:see?
I'd like...	**Ngingathanda...**
	ngeengaataa:ndaa...
We'd like...	**Singathanda...**
	seengaataa:ndaa...
I'd like an ice cream	**Ngingathanda u-ayisikhilimu**
	ngeengaataa:ndaa ooaa-yeeseeklee:moo
We'd like to visit Durban	**Singathanda ukuya eThekwini**
	seengaataa:ndaa oogoo:yaa etegwee:nee
some more.../ another	**-nye***
	-nye
some more bread	**esinye isinkwa**
	esee:nye eesee:nkwaa

some more soup	**elinye isobho**
	elee:nye eeso:bo
another coffee	**elinye ikhofi**
	elee:nye eeko:fee
another beer	**omunye ubhiya**
	omoo:nye oobee:yaa
How much is it?	**Yimalini?**
	yeemaalee:nee?
How much is the room?	**Limalini ikamelo?**
	leemaalee:nee eekaame:lo?
large/small	**-khulu, -ncane***
	-koo:loo, -ŋ/aa:ne
with/without	**na-, -ngena...***
	naa-, -ngenaa...
Where is/are...?	**-kuphi?***
	-koo:pee?
Where is the nearest...?	**-kuphi... -eduze?***
	-koo:pee... -edoo:ze?
Where are the nearest...?	**-kuphi... -eduze?**
	-koo:pee... -edoo:ze?
How do I get to the bus station?	**Ngifika kanjani esiteshini samabhasi?**
	ngeefee:gaa kaanjaa:nee esteshee:nee saamaabaa:see?
How do I get to Johannesburg?	**Ngifika kanjani eGoli?**
	ngeefee:gaa kaanjaa:nee ego:lee?
There is/are...	**Kukhona...**
	kooko:naa...
There isn't/aren't any ...	**Akukho...**
	aagoo:ko...

20

When...?	...**nini?**
	...nee:nee?
At what time...?	...**ngasikhathi sini?**
	...ngaaskaa:tee see:nee?
today	**namhlanje**
	naamɬaa:nje
tomorrow	**kusasa**
	koosaa:saa
Can I...?	**Nginga...?**
	ngeengaa...?
Can I smoke?	**Ngingabhema?**
	ngeengaabe:maa?
What does this mean?	**Kusho ukuthini lokhu?**
	koo:sho oogootee:nee lo:koo?

Polite expressions

The meal was delicious	**Ukudla bekwehla esiphundu**
	oogoo:ɓaa begwe:ɬaa espoo:ndoo
Thank you very much	**Ngiyabonga kakhulu**
	ngeeyaabo:ngaa kaakoo:loo
Delighted to meet you	**Ngijabulela ukukwazi**
	ngeejaaboole:laa oogoogwaa:zee
This is my husband	**Lona ngumyeni wami**
	lo:naa ngoomye:nee waa:mee
This is my wife	**Lena yinkosikazi yami**
	le:naa yeenkoseegaa:zee yaa:mee
Enjoy your holiday!	**Ube neholide elimnandi!**
	oo:be neholee:de eleemnaa:ndee!

Celebrations

• •

Both funerals and weddings have always been celebrated in a big way in the Zulu culture. Traditionally, wedding festivals stretched over a number of days and were attended by many people. Traditional beer formed an integral part of festivities.

I'd like to wish you a...	**Ngingathanda ukukufisela...** ngeengaataa:ndaa oogoogoofeese:laa...
Merry Christmas!	**uKhisimusi omuhle!** ookeeseemoo:see omoo:ɬe!
Happy New Year!	**uNyaka omusha omuhle!** oonyaa:gaa omoo:shaa omoo:ɬe!
Happy Easter!	**ama-Ista amahle!** aamaaee:staa aamaa:ɬe!
Happy Birthday!	**usuku oluhle lokuzalwa!** oosoo:goo oloo:ɬe logoozaa:lwaa!
Have a good trip!	**Ube nohambo oluhle!** oo:be nohaa:mbo oloo:ɬe!
Enjoy your meal!	**Ukujabulele ukudla!** oogoojaaboole:le oogoo:ɮaa!

Making friends

• •

Zulu personal names have meanings that are still known to the people. A typical name for a girl is **'Sibongile'** 'we are grateful', while a common name for a boy is **'Sibusiso'** 'blessing'. When you are talking to somebody, you use the name as it appears above, however, when you are referring to the person, you would say '**uSibongile**' or '**uSibusiso**'. You simply add the '**u-**' to the name.

How old are you?	**Uneminyaka emingaki?** oonemeenyaa:gaa emeengaa:gee?
I'm ... years old	**Ngineminyaka engu-...** ngeenemeenyaa:gaa engoo-...
Are you Zulu?	**UngumZulu?** oongoomzoo:loo?
I'm English/ Scottish/ American	**NgiyiNgisi, NgiyisiKoshi, NginguMmelikana** ngeeyeengee:see, ngeeyeesko:shee, ngeengoommelee:kaanaa
I'm from Pietermaritzburg	**Ngivela eMgungundlovu** ngeeve:laa emgoongoonǥo:voo
Where do you live? (singular)	**Uhlalaphi?** oo4aalaa:pee?
Where do you live? (plural)	**Nihlalaphi?** nee4aalaa:pee?
I live in Newcastle	**Ngihlala eNyukhasela** ngee4aa:laa enyookaase:laa
We live in Sidney	**Sihlala eSidney** see4aa:laa esidney
I'm single	**Angishadile** angeeshaadee:le
I'm married	**Ngishadile** ngeeshaadee:le

23

I'm divorced	**Ngidivosile**
	ngeedeevose:le
I have a boyfriend	**Nginalo isoka**
	ngeenaa:lo eeso:gaa
I have a girlfriend	**Nginayo intombi**
	ngeenaa:yo eento:mbee
I have a partner	**Nginaye umasihlalisane**
	ngeenaa:ye
	oomaasee4aaleesaa:ne
I have children	**Nginabo abantwana**
	ngeenaa:bo aabaantwaa:naa
I have no children	**Anginabo abantwana**
	aangeenaa:bo aabaantwaa:naa
I'm here on holiday	**Ngiseholideni**
	ngeeseholeede:nee
I'm here on business	**Ngenza ibhizinisi lapha**
	nge:ndzaa eebeezeenee:see laa:paa
I'm here for the weekend	**Ngilapha impelasonto**
	ngeelaa:paa eempelaaso:nto

FACE TO FACE

A **Ungubani igama lakho?**
oongoobaa:nee eegaa:maa laa:ko?
What's your name?

B **Igama lami nguJabulani**
eegaa:maa laa:mee ngoojaaboolaa:nee
My name is Jabulani

A **Udabukaphi?**
oodaaboogaa:pee?
Where are you from?

B **NgingumZulu, ngivela eMgungundlovu.**
ngeengoomzoo:loo, ngeeve:laa
   emgoongoonɓo:voo.
I am Zulu, from Pietermaritzburg.

A **Ngijabulela ukukwazi!**
ngeejaaboole:laa ogoogwaa:zee!
Pleased to meet you!

Work

What work do you do?	**Wenza msebenzi muni?** we:ndzaa msebe:ndzee moo:nee?
I'm a doctor	**Ngingudokotela** ngeengoodogote:laa
I'm a manager	**Ngingumphathi** ngeengoompaa:tee
I am a secretary	**Ngingunobhala** ngeengoonobaa:laa
I work from home	**Ngisebenza ekhaya** ngeesebe:ndzaa ekaa:yaa
I'm self-employed	**Ngiyazisebenza** ngeeyaazeesebe:ndzaa

Weather

It's sunny	**Libalele** leebaale:le
It's raining	**Liyana** leeyaa:naa

25

izulu eliguquguqukayo eezoo:loo eleegoo!ʔ oo-goo!ʔoogaa:yo	changeable weather
licwathile lee/ʔwaatee:le	fine
liyaduma leeyaadoo:maa	thundery weather

It's snowing **Liyakhithika**
leeyaakeetee:gaa

It's windy **Kunomoya**
koonomo:yaa

What a lovely day! **Ngusuku oluhle!**
ngoosoo:goo oloo:ɬe!

What awful weather! **Ngusuku olubi!**
ngoosoo:goo oloo:bee!

What will the weather be like tomorrow? **Isimo sezulu sizoba kanjani kusasa?**
eesee:mo sezoo:loo seezo:baa kaanjaa:nee koosaa:saa?

Do you think it's going to rain? **Uthi lizona kusasa?**
oo:tee leezo:naa koosaa:saa?

I need an umbrella **Ngidinga isambulela**
ngeedee:ngaa eesaamboole:laa

It's very hot **Kushisa kakhulu**
kooshee:saa kaakoo:loo

It's very cold **Kubanda kakhulu**
koobaa:ndaa kaakoo:loo

Do you think it will snow? **Uthi lizokhithika?**
oo:tee leezokeetee:gaa?

> **Leisure/interests** (p 70)

Getting around

Asking the way

malungana na..., ne..., no...* maaloongaa:naa naa..., ne..., no...	opposite
eceleni kwa..., kwe..., ko...* e/ʔele:nee kwaa..., kwe..., ko	next to
eduze na..., ne..., no...* edoo:ze naa..., ne..., no...	near to
impambano yemigwaqo eempaambaa:no yemeegwaa:!ʔo	crossroad
indingilizi eendeengeelee:zee	roundabout

We're looking for...	**Sifuna...** seefoo:naa...

Can we walk
   there?
	Singaya lapho ngezinyawo?
	 seengaa:yaa laa:po nge-
	   zeenyaa:wo?

We're lost	**Sidukile** seedoogee:le

27

Is this the right way to...?	**Yindlela efanele ukuya e...?**
	yeenʒe:laa efaane:le oogoo:yaa e...?
Can you show me on the map?	**Ungangikhombisa ebalazweni?**
	oongaangeekombee:saa ebaalaazwe:nee?

FACE TO FACE

A **Uxolo, ngifika kanjani esiteshini?**
oo//ʔo:lo, ngeefee:gaa kaanjaa:nee esteshee:nee?
Excuse me, how do I get to the station?

B **Qhubeka uqonde ngqo, ujikele ngakwesobunxele, ngakwesokudla ngemva kwebhange**
!hoobe:gaa oo!ʔo:nde ŋ!go, oojeege:le ngaagwesoboonɲɲe:le, ngagwesogoo:ɣaa nge:mvaa kwebaa:nge
Keep straight on, after the bank turn left/right

A **Kukude?**
koogoo:de?
Is it far?

B **Cha, amamitha angu-200, imizuzu engu-5**
/haa, aamaamee:taa aangoo200, eemeezoo:zoo engoo5
No, 200 metres/five minutes

A **A Ngiyabonga!**
ngeeyaabo:ngaa!
Thank you!

B **B Nami ngiyabonga!**
naa:mee ngeeyaabo:ngaa!
You're welcome!

Bus and coach

Is there a bus to...?	**Likhona ibhasi eliya e...?** leeko:naa eebaa:see elee:yaa e...?
Where do I catch the bus to go to...?	**Ngiligibela kuphi ibhasi eliya e...?** ngeeleegeebe:laa koo:pee eebaa:see elee:ya e...?
How much is it to...?	**Yimalini ukuya e...?** yeemaalee:nee oogoo:yaa e...?
How much is it to the centre?	**Yimalini ukuya enkabeni yedolobha?** yeemaalee:nee oogoo:yaa enkaabe:nee yedolo:baa?
How much is it to the beach?	**Yimalini ukuya ebhishi?** yeemaalee:nee oogoo:yaa ebee:shee?
How much is it to the Waterfront?	**Yimalini ukuya eWaterfront?** yeemaalee:nee oogoo:yaa ewaterfront?

FACE TO FACE

A **Uxolo, yiliphi ibhasi eliya enkabeni yedolobha?**
oo//ʔo:lo, yeelee:pee eebaa:see elee:yaa enkaabe:nee yedolo:baa?
Excuse me, which bus goes to the centre?

B **Unamba 15**
oonaa:mbaa 15
Number 15

A **Sikuphi isitobhu samabhasi?**
seegoo:pee eesto:boo saamaabaa:see?
Where is the bus stop?

B **Laphaya, ngakwesobunxele**
laapaa:yaa, ngaagwesoboon//e:le
There, on the left

A **Ngingawathengaphi amathikithi ebhasi?**
ngeengaawaatengaa:pee aamaateegee:tee ebaa:see?
Where can I buy bus tickets?

B **Laphaya, emshinini wamathikithi**
laapaa:yaa, emsheenee:nee waamaateegee:tee
Over there, at the ticket machine

How often are the buses to...?	**Amabhasi aya e... ahamba kangaki?** aamaabaa:see aa:yaa e... aahaa:mbaa kaangaa:gee?
When is the first/ the last bus to...?	**Ibhasi lokuqala, lokugcina eliya e... lihamba ngasikhathi sini?** eebaa:see logoo!ʔaa:laa, logoo-/ġee:naa elee:yaa e... leehaa:-mbaa ngaaskaa:tee see:nee?

Could you tell me when to get off?	**Ungangitshela ukuthi ngehle kuphi?**
	oongaangeeche:laa oogoo:tee nge:4e koo:pee?
This is my stop	**Ngifanele ngehle lapha**
	ngeefaane:le nge:4e laa:paa

Train

· ·

Trains in South Africa can roughly be divided into the following categories: affordable urban commuter trains, affordable long-distance trains, luxury trains and novelty trains. While commuter trains are not always a good travelling option for tourists, travel on the other trains can be an unforgettable experience. The long-distance Shosholoza Meyl is a comfortable and affordable alternative to the very luxurious Blue Train and Rovos Rail.

First class	**Ufesikilasi**
	oofeseekeelaa:see
Second class	**Usekenikilasi**
	oosegeneekeelaa:see
Smoking	**Kubhenywa lapha**
	koobe:nywaa laa:paa
Non-smoking	**Akubhenywa lapha**
	aagoobe:nywaa laa:paa
Is there a supplement to pay?	**Ngifanele ngikhokhe iseleko?**
	ngeefaane:le ngeeko:ke eesele:go?

> **Luggage** (p 88)

uhlelo lwezikhathi	timetable
oo⁴e:lo lwezeekaa:tee	
-hamba* -haa:mbaa	to operate
ngamaSonto nangamaholide	Sundays and holidays
ngaamaaso:nto naangaamaaholee:de	
emapulatifomu emaapoolateefo:moo	to the platforms

Getting around

I want to book a seat on the Apple Express	**Ngifuna ukubhuka isihlalo e-Apple Express** ngeefoo:naa oogooboo:gaa ees⁴aa:lo eapple express
When is the train to...?	**Isitimela esiya e ... sihamba ngasikhathi sini?** eesteeme:laa esee:yaa e ... seehaa:mbaa ngaaskaa:tee see:nee?
When is the first train to...?	**Isitimela sokuqala esiya e ... sihamba ngasikhathi sini?** eesteeme:laa sogoo!ʔaa:laa esee:yaa e ... seehaa:mbaa ngaaskaa:tee see:nee?
When is the last train to...?	**Isitimela sokugcina esiya e ... sihamba ngasikhathi sini?** eesteeme:laa sogoo/ġee:naa esee:yaa e ... seehaa:mbaa ngaaskaa:tee see:nee?
When does it arrive in...?	**Sifika e ... ngasikhathi sini?** seefee:gaa e ... ngaaskaa:tee see:nee?

Do I have to change?	**Kufanele ngishintshe ngigibele esinye isitimela?**
	koofaane:le ngeeshee:nche ngeegeebe:le esee:nye eesteeme:laa?
Which platform does it leave from?	**Sima kuliphi ipulatifomu?**
	see:maa koolee:pee epoolateefo:moo?
Is this the right platform for the train to Pretoria?	**Yipulatifomu elifanele yini leli lokugibela isitimela esiya ePitoli?**
	yeepoolateefo:moo eleefaane:le yee:nee le:lee logoogeebe:laa eesteeme:laa esee:yaa epeeto:lee?
Is this the train for...?	**Ingabe lesi yisitimela esiya e...?**
	eengaa:be le:see yeesteeme:laa esee:yaa e...?
When does it leave?	**Sihamba ngasikhathi sini?**
	seehaa:mbaa ngaaskaa:tee see:nee?
Does the train stop at...?	**Ingabe isitimela sima e...?**
	eengaa:be eesteeme:laa see:maa e...?
Where do I change for...?	**Ngisigibela kuphi isitimela esiya e...?**
	ngeeseegeebe:laa koo:pee eesteeme:laa esee:yaa e...?
Please tell me when we get to...	**Ngicela ungitshele uma sifika e...**
	ngee/ʔe:laa oongeeche:le oo:maa seefee:gaa e...

Train

33

Where do I collect prepaid tickets from?	**Ngiwalanda kuphi amathikithi akhokhelwa kusengaphambili?**
	ngeewaalaa:ndaa koo:pee amaateegee:tee aakoke:lwaa koosengaapaambee:lee?
Is this seat free?	**Ngingahlala lapha?**
	ngeengaa‡aa:laa laa:paa?
Excuse me	**Uxolo!**
	oo//ʔo:lo!
Sorry!	**Nxese!**
	ŋ//e:se!

FACE TO FACE

A **Isitimela esilandelayo esiya e ... sifika ngasikhathi sini?**
eesteeme:laa eseelaandelaa:yo esee:yaa e ... seefee:gaa ngaaskaa:tee see:nee?
When is the next train to...?

B **Ngo-5.10**
ngo5.10
At ten past five

A **Amathikithi amabili ukuya e...**
amaateegee:tee amaabee:lee oogoo:yaa e...
Two tickets to...

B **Isingili noma irentheni?**
eeseengee:lee no:maa eereete:nee?
Single or return?

A **Ngicela irentheni**
ngee/ʔe:laa eereete:nee
Return please

Taxi

irenke yamatekisi eere:nke yaamaategee:see	taxi rank

I want a taxi	**Ngifuna itekisi** ngeefoo:naa eetegee:see
Where can I get a taxi?	**Ngingaligibela kuphi itekisi?** ngeengaaleegeebe:laa koo:pee eetegee:see?
Could you order me a taxi?	**Ungangifunela itekisi?** oongaangeefoone:laa eetegee:see?
How much is it going to cost to go to...?	**Yimalini ukuya e...?** yeemaalee:nee oogoo:yaa e...?
to the town centre	**enkabeni yedolobha** enkaabe:nee yedolo:baa
to the station	**esiteshini** esteshee:nee
to the airport	**esikhumulweni sezindiza** eskoomoolwe:nee sezeendee:zaa
to this address	**kuleli kheli** koole:lee ke:lee
How much is it?	**Yimalini?** yeemaalee:nee?
It's more than on the meter	**Kubiza ngaphezu kokuboniswe emitheni** koobee:zaa ngaape:zoo kokoobonee:swe emeete:nee

35

Keep the change	**Gcina ushintshi**
	/ĝee:naa ooshee:nchee
Sorry, I don't have any change	**Ngiyaxolisa, anginawo ushintshi**
	ngeeyaa//ʔolee:saa, angeenaa:wo ooshee:nchee
I'm in a hurry	**Ngijahile**
	ngeejaahee:le
Is it far?	**Kukude?**
	koogoo:de?

Boat and ferry

When is the next boat/ferry to...?	**Isikebhe, isikebhe sokuweza esilandelayo esiya e ... sihamba ngasikhathi sini?**
	eeske:be, eeske:be sogoowe:-zaa eseelaandelaa:yo esee:yaa e ... seehaa:mbaa ngaaskaa:tee see:nee?
Have you a timetable?	**Unalo yini uhlelo lwezikhathi?**
	oonaalo yee:nee oo⁴e:lo lwezeekaa:tee?
Is there a car ferry to...?	**Sikhona yini isikebhe esithutha izimoto esiya e...?**
	seeko:naa yee:nee eeske:be esee-too:taa eezeemo:to esee:yaa e...?
How much is...?	**Yimalini...?**
	yeemaalee:nee...?
a single	**isingili**
	eeseengee:lee

a return	**iritheni**
	eereete:nee
a tourist ticket	**ithikithi lesihambi**
	eeteegee:tee leshaa:mbee
How much is it for a car and ... people?	**Yimalini ukuthatha imoto nabantu abangu-...?**
	yeemaalee:nee ogootaa:taa eemo:to naabaa:ntoo abaangoo-...?
How long is the crossing?	**Ukuwela kuthatha isikhathi esingakanani?**
	oogoowe:laa kootaa:taa eeskaa:tee eseengaagaanaa:-nee?
Where does the boat leave from?	**Isikebhe sisukela kuphi?**
	eeske:be seesooge:laa koo:pee?
When is the first/last boat?	**Isikebhe sokuqala, sokugcina sihamba ngasikhathi sini?**
	eske:be sogoo!ʔaa:laa, sogoo-/ǥee:naa seehaa:mbaa ngaaskaa:tee see:nee?
What time do we get to...?	**Sifika e ... ngasikhathi sini?**
	seefee:gaa e ... ngaaskaa:tee see:nee?
Is there somewhere to eat on the boat?	**Ikhona indawo yokudlela esikebheni?**
	eeko:naa eendaa:wo yogooʒe:-laa eskebe:nee?

Air travel

- -

How do I get to the airport?	**Ngihamba kanjani ukuya esikhumulweni sezindiza?**
	ngeehaa:mbaa kaanjaa:nee oogoo:yaa eskoomoolwe:nee sezeendee:zaa?
How long does it take to get to the airport?	**Kuthatha isikhathi esingakanani ukuya esikhumulweni sezindiza?**
	kootaa:taa eeskaa:tee eseengaagaanaa:nee oogoo:yaa eskoomoolwe:nee sezeendee:zaa?
How much is the taxi fare into town?	**Yimalini ukuya edolobheni ngetekisi?**
	yeemaalee:nee oogoo:yaa edolobe:nee ngetegee:see?
How much is the taxi fare to the hotel?	**Yimalini ukuya ehhotela ngetekisi?**
	yeemaalee:nee oogoo:yaa ehote:laa ngetegee:see?
Is there an airport bus to the city centre?	**Likhona yini ibhasi lasesikhumulweni sezindiza eliya enkabeni yedolobha?**
	leeko:naa yee:nee eebaa:see laaseskoomoolwe:nee sezeendee:zaa elee:yaa enkaabe:nee yedolo:baa?

Where do I check in for...?	**Ngifanele ngingene kuphi ukuya e...?**
	ngeefaane:le ngeenge:ne koo:pee oogoo:yaa e...?
Where is the luggage for the flight from...?	**Ukuphi umthwalo webhanoyi elivela e...?**
	oogoo:pee oomtwaa:loo webaano:yee eleeve:laa e...?
Which is the departure gate for the flight to...?	**Ungena kuliphi isango uma ufuna ibhanoyi eliya e...?**
	oonge:naa koolee:pee eesaa:ngo oo:maa oofoo:naa eebaano:yee elee:yaa e...?

YOU MAY HEAR...

Ufanele ukugibela esangweni elithi... oofaane:le oogoogeebe:laa esaangwe:nee elee:tee...	Boarding will take place at gate number...
Phuthumela esangweni elithi... pootoome:laa esaangwe:nee elee:tee...	Go immediately to gate number...
Ibhanoyi lakho libambekile eebaano:yee laa:ko leebaambegee:le	Your flight is delayed

Air travel

> **Luggage** (p 88)

Customs control

International airports in South Africa normally have one channel for South African passport holders and another for foreign passport holders. There are also 'declare goods' and 'nothing to declare' channels. Officials sometimes carry out random baggage searches.

indawo yokuhlolwa kwamaphasipothi eendaa:wo yogoo4o:lwaa kwaamaapaaseepo:tee	passport control
uphiko lwezezintela oopee:go lwezezeente:laa	customs

Do I have to pay duty on this?	**Kufanele ngikukhokhele intela lokhu?** koofaane:le ngeegookoke:le eente:laa lo:koo?
It is for my own personal use	**Ngikufunela mina luqobo** ngeegoofoone:laa mee:naa loo!ʔo:bo

Driving

Car hire

ilayisense yokushayela eelaayeese:ntse yogooshaaye:laa	driving licence
umshuwalense oomshoowaale:ntse	insurance

I want to hire a car	**Ngifuna ukuqasha imoto** ngeefoo:naa oogoo!ʔaa:shaa eemo:to
I want to hire a car for … days	**Ngifuna ukuqasha imoto izinsuku ezingu-…** ngeefoo:naa oogoo!ʔaa:shaa eemo:to eezeentsoo:goo ezeengoo…
I want to hire a car for the weekend	**Ngifuna ukuqasha imoto impelasonto** ngeefoo:naa oogoo!ʔaa:shaa eemo:to eempelaaso:nto
What are your rates per day?	**Yimalini ngosuku?** yeemaalee:nee ngosoo:goo?

41

What are your rates per week?	**Yimalini ngesonto?** yeemaalee:nee ngeso:nto?
Is there a mileage (km) charge?	**Ukhokha ngekhilomitha?** ooko:kaa ngekeelomee:taa?
How much is it?	**Yimalini?** yeemaalee:nee?
Does the price include comprehensive insurance?	**Ingabe leli nani lihlanganisa nomshuwalense ogcwele?** eengaa:be le:lee naa:nee lee╪aangaanee:saa nomshoo-waale:ntse o/ġwe:le?
Must I return the car here?	**Ngiyibuyisele lapha lapha?** ngeeyeebooyeese:le laa:paa laa:paa?
By what time?	**Ngasikhathi sini?** ngaaskaa:tee see:nee?
I'd like to leave it in...	**Ngingathanda ukuyishiya e...** ngeengaataa:ndaa ogooyeeshee:yaa e...
What do I do if we break down?	**Kufanele ngenzeni uma imoto ifa?** koofaane:le ngendze:nee oo:maa eemo:to ee:faa?

YOU MAY HEAR...

Ngicela ubuyise imoto inophetilomu ogcwele ngee/ʔe:laa oobooyee:se eemo:to eenopeteelo:moo o/ġwe:le	Please return the car with a full tank

42

Driving

I am looking for a car park	**Ngifuna indawo yokupaka izimoto**
	ngeefoo:naa eendaa:wo yogoopaa:gaa eezeemo:to
Do I need to pay?	**Kudingeka ngikhokhe?**
	koodeenge:gaa ngeeko:ke?
Can I park here?	**Ngingapaka lapha?**
	ngeengaapaa:gaa laa:paa?
How long can I park for?	**Ngingapaka isikhathi esingakanani?**
	ngeengaapaa:gaa eeskaa:tee eseengaagaanaa:nee?
Is the road good?	**Muhle lo mgwaqo?**
	moo:ɬe lo mgwaa:!ʔo?
Can you show me on the map?	**Ungangikhombisa ebalazweni?**
	oongaangeekombee:saa ebaalaazwe:nee?

Petrol

i-unleaded	eeunleaded	unleaded
udizili	oodeezee:lee	diesel

Fill it up, please	**Ngicela uwugcwalise**
	ngee/ʔe:laa oowoo/ġwaalee:se
Please check the oil	**Ngicela uhlole uwoyela**
	ngee/ʔe:laa ooɬo:le oowoye:laa

Please check the water	**Ngicela uhlole amanzi** ngee/ʔe:laa ooɬo:le amaa:ndzee
...South African Rand' worth of unleaded petrol	**i-unleaded yamarandi angu-...** eeunleaded yaamaaraa:ndee aangoo...
Pump number...	**Iphampu ethi...** eepaa:mpoo e:tee...
Can you check the tyre pressure?	**Ungangihlolela umoya?** oongaangeeɬole:laa oomo:yaa?
Where do I pay?	**Kufanele ngikhokhe kuphi?** koofaane:le ngeeko:ke koo:pee?
Do you take credit cards?	**Niyayamukela i-credit card?** neeyaayaamooge:laa eecredit card?

Breakdown

usizo lokudonswa kwemoto oosee:zo logoodo:ntswa kwemo:to	breakdown assistance

Can you help me?	**Ungangisiza?** oongaangeesee:zaa?
My car has broken down	**Ngiphukelwe yimoto** ngeepooge:lwe yeemo:to
I can't start the car	**Imoto ayifuni ukuduma** eemo:to aayeefoo:nee oogoodoo:maa

I've run out of petrol	**Imoto yami iphelelwe nguphetilomu**
	eemo:to yaa:mee eepele:lwe ngoopeteelo:moo
Is there a garage near here?	**Kukhona igalaji eliseduze?**
	kooko:naa eegalaa:jee eleesedoo:ze?
Can you tow me to the nearest garage?	**Ungangidonsela egalaji eliseduze?**
	oongaangeedontse:laa egaalaa:jee eleesedoo:ze?
Do you have parts for a (Toyota)?	**Ninazo izipele ze(Toyota)?**
	neenaa:zo eezeepe:le ze(toyota)?
There's something wrong with the... (see Car parts)	**Kukhona inkinga nga..., nge..., ngo...** *
	kooko:naa eenkee:ngaa ngaa..., nge..., ngo...

Car parts

• •

The ... doesn't work	Negative + **-sebenzi***
	...sebe:ndzee
The ... don't work	Negative + **-sebenzi***
	...sebe:ndzee

accelerator	**amafutha**	aamaafoo:taa
battery	**ibhethri**	eebe:tree
bonnet	**ibhonethi**	eebone:tee
brakes	**amabhuleki**	aamaaboole:gee

choke	**ishoki**	eesho:gee
clutch	**ikilashi**	eekeelaa:shee
distributor	**idistributha**	eedeestreeboo:-taa
engine	**injini**	eenjee:nee
exhaust pipe	**i-okzozo**	eeokzo:zo
fuse	**ifiyuzi**	eefeeyoo:zee
gears	**amagiya**	aamaagee:yaa
handbrake	**ihendibhrekhi**	eehendeebre:kee
headlights	**izibani zangaphambili**	eezeebaa:nee zaangaapaa-mbee:lee
ignition	**i-ignishini**	ee-eegneeshee:nee
indicator	**i-indikhetha**	ee-eendeeke:taa
points	**amaphoyinti**	aamaapoyee:ntee
radiator	**irediyetha**	iredeeye:taa
reversing lights	**izibani zokuhlehla**	eezeebaa:nee zogoo4e:4aa
seat belt	**ibhande lokuphepha**	eebaa:nde logoope:paa
sidelights	**izibane eziseceleni**	eezeebaa:ne ezeese/ʔele:nee
spare wheel	**isondo eliyisipele**	eeso:ndo eleeyeespe:le
spark plugs	**spaki pulaki**	spaa:kee poolaa:-kee
steering	**isteringi**	eesteree:ngee
steering wheel	**isteringi**	eesteree:ngee
tyre	**ithayi**	eetaa:yee
wheel	**isondo**	eeso:ndo

windscreen	**iwindiskrini**	eeweendeeskree:-nee
windscreen washers	**amawasha ewindiskrini**	aamaawaa:shaa eweendeeskree:-nee
windscreen wiper	**amawayipha**	aamaawaayee:paa

Staying somewhere

Hotel (booking)

a single room	**ikamelo eliyisingili**
	eekaame:lo eleeyeeseengee:lee
a double room	**ikamelo eliyidabuli**
	eekaame:lo eleeyeedaaboo:lee
with bath	**elinobhavu**
	eleenobaa:voo
with shower	**elineshawa**
	eleeneshaa:waa
with a double bed	**elinombhede oyidabuli**
	eleenombe:de oyeedaaboo:lee
twin-bedded	**elinemibhede emibili**
	eleenemeebe:de emeebee:lee
with an extra bed for a child	**elinombhede omunye womntwana**
	eleenombe:de omoo:nye womntwaa:naa
I'd like (to book) a single room	**Ngingathanda ukubhuka ikamelo eliyisingili**
	ngeengaataa:ndaa ogooboo:gaa eekaame:lo eleeyeeseengee:lee
I'd like (to book) a double room	**Ngingathanda ukubhuka ikamelo eliyidabuli**

48

	ngeengaataa:ndaa ogooboo:gaa eekaame:lo eleeyeedaaboo:lee
For one night	**Usuku ololodwa**
	oosoo:goo oloolo:dwaa
For ... nights	**Izinsuku ezingu-...**
	eezeentsoo:goo ezeengoo...
From... till...	**Kusuka kumhla ka-... kuya kumhla ka-...**
	koosoo:gaa koo:m4aa kaa... koo:yaa koo:m4aa kaa...
For how many people?	**Abantu abangaki?**
	aabaa:ntoo aabaangaa:gee?
For one person	**Umuntu oyedwa**
	oomoo:ntoo oye:dwaa
For ... people	**Abantu abangu-...**
	aabaa:ntoo aabaangoo...
How much is it per night?	**Yimalini ngosuku?**
	yeemaalee:nee ngosoo:goo?
How much is it per week?	**Yimalini ngesonto?**
	yeemaalee:nee ngeso:nto?
Do you have a room for tonight?	**Ngingalithola ikamelo namhlanje kusihlwa?**
	ngeengaaleeto:laa eekaame:lo nam4aa:nje koosee:4waa?
I'll arrive at...	**Ngizofika ngo-...**
	ngeezofee:gaa ngo...
Do you have a list of hotels with prices?	**Unalo uhlu lwamahhotela namanani awo?**
	oonaa:lo oo:4oo lwaamaahote:- laa naamaanaa:nee aa:wo?

Could you recommend a good hotel?	**Yiliphi ihhotela elingcono olaziyo?**
	yeelee:pee eehote:laa eleen/go:no olaazee:yo?
Could you recommend a hotel that is not too expensive?	**Yiliphi ihhotela elibiza kahle olaziyo?**
	yeelee:pee eehote:laa eleebee:zaa kaa:ɬe olaazee:yo?

YOU MAY HEAR...

Sigcwele	We're full
see/ġwe:le	
Ngicela igama lakho?	Your name, please?
ngee/ʔe:laa eegaa:maa laa:ko?	
Izinsuku ezingaki?	For how many nights?
eezeeentsoo:goo ezeengaa:gee?	
Sicela uqiniseke nge-e-mail	Please confirm by e-mail
see/ʔe:laa ooǃʔeeneese:ge nge:email	
Sicela uqiniseke ngesikhahlamezi	Please confirm by fax
see/ʔe:laa ooǃʔeeneese:ge ngeskaaɬaame:zee	
Uzofika ngasikhathi sini?	What time will you arrive?
oozofee:gaa ngaaskaa:tee see:nee?	

50

Hotel desk

I booked a room	**Ngabhuke ikamelo**
	ngaaboo:ge eekaame:lo
My name is...	**Igama lami ngu...**
	eegaa:maa laa:mee ngoo...
Have you anything else?	**Unalo elinye ikamelo?**
	oonaa:lo elee:nye eekaame:lo?
Where can I park the car?	**Ngingayipaka kuphi imoto yami?**
	ngeengaayeepaa:gaa koo:pee eemo:to yaa:mee?
What time is dinner?	**Ukudla kwakusihlwa kudliwa ngasikhathi sini?**
	oogoo:ɮaa kwaagoosee:ɬwaa gooɮee:waa ngaaskaa:tee see:nee?
What time is breakfast?	**Ibhulakufesi lidliwa ngasikhathi sini?**
	eeboolagoofe:see leeɮee:waa ngaaskaa:tee see:nee?
The key, please	**Ngicela isikhiye**
	ngee/ˀe:laa eeskee:ye
Room number...	**Inombolo yekamelo ithi...**
	eenombo:lo yekaame:lo ee:tee...
I'm leaving tomorrow	**Ngihamba kusasa**
	ngeehaa:mbaa goosaa:saa
Please prepare the bill	**Ngicela ulungise imali yokukhokha**
	ngee/ˀe:laa ooloongee:se eemaa:lee yogooko:kaa

51

Camping

Staying somewhere

izibi eezee:bee	rubbish
amanzi okuphuza aamaa:ndzee ogoopoo:zaa	drinking water
amashawa aamaashaa:waa	washing facilities

Is there a restaurant on the campsite?
Kukhona yini isitolo sokudlela endaweni yokukhempa?
kooko:naa yee:nee eesto:lo sogooǥe:laa endaawe:nee yogooke:mpaa?

Do you have any vacancies?
Zikhona yini izikhala zomsebenzi?
zeeko:naa yee:nee eezeekaa:laa zomsebe:ndzee?

Does the price include hot water?
Ingabe leli nani lihlanganisa namanzi ashisayo?
eengaa:be le:lee naa:nee lee꜀aangaanee:saa naamaa:ndzee aasheesaa:yo?

Does the price include electricity?
Ingabe leli nani lihlanganisa nogesi?
eengaa:be le:lee naa:nee lee꜀aangaanee:saa noge:see?

We'd like to stay for ... nights
Singathanda ukuhlala ubusuku obungu-...
seengaataa:ndaa oogoo꜀aa:laa ooboosoo:goo oboongoo...

52

How much is it per night for a tent?	**Libiza malini ithende ubusuku ngabunye?**
	leebee:zaa maalee:nee eete:nde ooboosoo:goo ngaaboo:nye?
How much is it per night for a caravan?	**Ibiza malini ikharavani ubusuku ngabunye?**
	eebee:zaa maalee:nee eekarava:nee ooboosoo:goo ngaaboo:nye?

Self-catering

South Africa has a wide variety of self-catering accommodation.

Who do we contact if there are problems?	**Sithintana nobani uma kukhona izinkinga?**
	seeteentaa:naa nobaa:nee oomaa kooko:naa eezeenkee:ngaa?
How does the heating work?	**Ukufudumeza kusebenza kanjani?**
	oogoofoodoome:zaa koosebe:ndzaa kaanjaa:nee?
Is there always hot water?	**Awapheli amanzi ashisayo?**
	aawaape:lee aamaa:ndzee aasheesaa:yo?
Where is the nearest supermarket?	**Isuphamakhethe eliseduze likuphi?**
	eesoopamaake:te eleesedoo:ze leegoo:pee?
Where do we leave the rubbish?	**Sizilahlaphi izibi?**
	seezeelaa4aa:pee eezee:bee?

53

Shopping

During the week, shops usually open from 8–9 am until 5–7 pm. On Saturdays some close earlier, while others remain open until late. Many shops also open on Sundays.

Shopping phrases

FACE TO FACE

A **Ungathandani?**
oongaataandaa:nee?
What would you like?

B **Una...**(one person), **Nina...** (more than one person)*
oonaa..., neenaa...
Do you have...?

A **Yebo, ngokuqinisekile. Kukhona okunye engingakusiza ngakho?**
ye:bo, ngogoo!ʔeeneesegee:le. kooko:naa ogoo:nye engeengaagoosee:zaa ngaa:ko?
Yes, certainly. Here you are. Anything else?

Where is...?	**...kuphi?***
	...goo:pee?
I'm looking for a present for...	**Ngifuna ukuthengela u ... isipho**
	ngeefoo:naa oogootenge:laa
	oo ... eesee:po

I'm looking for a present for my mother	**Ngifuna ukuthengela umama isipho**
	ngeefoo:naa oogootenge:laa oomaa:maa eesee:po
I'm looking for a present for a child	**Ngifuna ukuthengela umntwana isipho**
	ngeefoo:naa oogootenge:laa oomntwaa:naa eesee:po
Where can I buy...?	**Ngingathengaphi...?**
	ngeengaatengaa:pee...?
Where can I buy gifts?	**Ngingazithengaphi izipho?**
	ngeengaazeetengaa:pee eezee:poo?
Where is the ... department?	**Kukuphi lapho kuthengiswa khona...?**
	koogoo:pee laa:po kootengee:swaa ko:naa...?
Where is the perfume dept?	**Athengiswaphi amakha?**
	aatengeeswaa:pee aamaa:kaa?
Where is the jewellery department?	**Athengiswaphi amajuweli?**
	aatengeeswaa:pee aamaajoowe:lee?
I'd like something similar to this	**Ngingathanda into efana nale**
	ngeengaataa:ndaa ee:nto efaa:naa naa:le
It's too expensive for me	**Kubiza kakhulu**
	koobee:zaa kaakoo:loo
Have you anything else?	**Ninokunye?**
	neenogoo:nye?

Shops

●●●

| **isitolo** eesto:lo | shop |
| **indali** eendaa:lee | sale |

buy one get one free	**thenga okukodwa uthole okunye mahhala** te:ngaa ogoogo:dwaa ooto:le ogoo:nye maahaa:laa
the food department	**lapho kuthengiswa khona ukudla** laa:po kootengee:swaa ko:naa oogoo:ƙaa
bakery	**ibhikawozi** eebeegaawo:zee
bookshop	**isitolo sezincwadi** eesto:lo sezeeŋ/waa:dee
butchery	**isilaha** eeslaa:haa
clothes shop	**isitolo sezingubo** eesto:lo sezeengoo:bo
Delicatessen shop	**isitolo sokudla kwekhethelo** eesto:lo sogoo:ƙaa kwekete:lo
DIY/hardware shop	**i-DIY, hardware shop** eediy, hardware shop
dry-cleaner's	**ilondolo** eelondo:lo
furniture shop	**isitolo sefenisha** eesto:lo sefenee:shaa
gift shop	**isitolo sezipho** eesto:lo sezee:po

56

greengrocer's	**isitolo semifino nezithelo**
	eesto:lo semeefee:no nezeete:lo
grocer's	**isitolo sokudla**
	eesto:lo sogoo:ɮaa
hairdresser's	**olungisa izinwele**
	oloongee:saa eezeenwe:le
health food shop	**isitolo sokudla okunempilo**
	eesto:lo sogoo:ɮaa ogoonempee:lo
hypermarket	**ihayiphamakethe**
	eehaayeepamaake:te
jeweller's	**isitolo samagugu okuhloba**
	eesto:lo saamaagoo:goo ogooɬo:baa
market	**imakethe**
	eemaake:te
perfume shop	**isitolo samaphefiyumi**
	eesto:lo saamaapefeeyoo:mee
pharmacy/ chemist's	**ikhemisi**
	eekemee:see
self-service	**uyaziseva**
	ooyaazeese:vaa
shoe shop	**isitolo sezicathulo**
	eesto:lo sezee/ʔaatoo:lo
sports shop	**isitolo sezemidlalo**
	eesto:lo sezemeeɮaa:lo
stationery shop	**isitolo sezidingo zokubhala**
	eesto:lo sezeedee:ngo zogoobaa:laa
sweet shop	**isitolo samaswidi**
	eesto:lo saamaaswee:dee
supermarket	**isuphamakhethe**
	eesoopamaake:te

tobacconist's	**othengisa ngogwayi**
	otengee:saa ngogwaa:yee
toy shop	**isitolo samathoyizi**
	eesto:lo saamaatoyee:zee

Handicrafts and art

South Africa has beautiful handicrafts and indigenous art on offer. These items can be purchased at reasonable prices at arts and crafts markets, flea markets, roadside stalls and tourist spots. There are also many curio shops scattered across the country.

Where can I buy curios?	**Ngingawathengaphi amaqabuqabu?**
	ngeengaawaatengaa:pee aamaa!ʔaaboo!ʔaa:boo?
Do you sell indigenous art?	**Niyabuthengisa yini ubuciko bomdabu?**
	neeyaabootengee:saa yee:nee ooboo/ʔee:go bomdaa:boo?
I would like to buy...	**Ngingathanda ukuthenga...**
	ngeengaataa:ndaa oogoote:ngaa...
a clay beer pot	**ukhamba**
	ookaa:mbaa
a drum	**isigubhu**
	eesgoo:boo
a carving	**into ebaziwe**
	ee:nto ebaazee:we

beadwork	okwenziwe ngobuhlalu	
	ogwe:ndzee:we ngoboo‡aa:loo	
a knobkerrie	isagila	
	eesaagee:laa	
a reed mat	icansi	
	ee/ʔaa:ntsee	
a shield	ihawu	
	eehaa:woo	

Food (general)

bread	isinkwa	eesee:nkwaa
bread (brown)	isinkwa	eesee:nkwaa
	esinsundu	eseentsoo:ndoo
bread roll	ibhanisi	eebaanee:see
butter	ibhotela	eebote:laa
cheese	ushizi	ooshee:zee
chicken	inyama	eenyaa:maa
	yenkukhu	yenkoo:koo
coffee (instant)	ikhofi	eeko:fee
cream	ukhilimu	ookeelee:moo
crisps/chips	amashibusi	aamaasheeboo:see
eggs	amaqanda	aamaa!ʔaa:ndaa
fish	inhlanzi	een‡aa:ndzee
flour	ufulawa	oofoolaa:waa
ham (cooked)	umlenze	oomle:ndze
	wengulube	wengooloo:be
	ophekiwe	opegee:we
ham (cured)	umlenze	oomle:ndze
	wengulube	wengooloo:be
	ogqunyisiwe	o!ǂoonyeesee:we

59

herbal tea	**itiye lamakhambi**	eetee:ye laamaakaa:mbee
honey	**uju**	oo:joo
jam	**ujamu**	oojaa:moo
margarine	**imajarini**	eemaajaaree:nee
marmalade	**imamaledi**	eemaamaale:dee
milk	**ubisi**	oobee:see
mustard	**umastadi**	oomaastaa:dee
oil	**amafutha**	aamaafoo:taa
orange juice	**ujusi wama-wolintshi**	oojoo:see waamaawolee:-nchee
pasta	**iphasta**	eepaa:staa
pepper	**upelepele**	oopelepe:le
rice	**irayisi**	eeraayee:see
salt	**usawoti**	oosaawo:tee
sugar	**ushukela**	ooshooge:laa
stock cube	**i-stock cube**	eestock cube
tea	**itiye**	eetee:ye
tin of tomatoes	**ithini likatamatisi**	eetee:nee leegaataamaatee:-see
vinegar	**uvinika**	ooveenee:gaa
yoghurt	**iyogathi**	eeyogaa:tee

Food (fruit and veg)

Fruit

| fruit | **izithelo** | eezeete:lo |
| apples | **ama-apula** | aamaa-aapoo:laa |

apricots	**amabhilikosi**	aamaabeeleeko:see
bananas	**obhanana**	obaanaa:naa
cherries	**amasheri**	aamaashe:ree
grapefruit	**ipapamuzi**	eepaapaamoo:zee
grapes	**amagilebhisi**	aamaageelebee:see
lemon	**ulamula**	oolaamoo:laa
nectarines	**amanektharini**	aamaanektaaree:nee
oranges	**amawolintshi**	aamaawolee:nchee
peaches	**amapetshisi**	aamaapeche:see
pears	**amaganandoda**	aamaagaanaando:- daa
pineapple	**uphayinaphu**	opaayeenaa:poo
plums	**amapulamu**	aamaapoolaa:moo
raspberries	**amajikijolo**	aamaajeegeejo:lo
strawberries	**amasitrobheri**	aamaastrobe:ree
watermelons	**amakhabe**	aamaakaa:be

Vegetables

vegetables	**imifino**	eemeefee:no
asparagus	**i-asparagasi**	eeasparaga:see
beans	**ubhontshisi**	oobonchee:see
carrots	**izaqathe**	eezaaǃʔaa:te
cauliflower	**ukholifulawa**	ookoleefoolaa:waa
courgettes/ baby marrows	**amagawu amancane**	aamaagaa:woo aamaaŋ/aa:ne
garlic	**ugalikhi**	oogaalee:kee
leeks	**amashaladi amakhulu**	aamaashaalaa:dee aamaakoo:loo
lettuce	**uletisi**	ooletee:see

61

mushrooms	amakhowa	aar..ako:waa
onions	u-anyanisi	ooaanyaanee:see
peas	uphizi	oopee:zee
peppers	uphepha	oope:paa
potatoes	amazambane	aamaazaambaa:ne
spinach	ispinashi	eespeenaa:shee
tomatoes	utamatisi	ootaamaatee:see

Clothes

Although sizes will always vary slightly, South African shoe and clothing sizes are normally the same as UK sizes. Clothing is also sometimes marked S, M, L, XL etc.

May I try this on?	**Ngingakulinganisa?**
	ngeengaagooleengaanee:saa?
Do you have it in	**Unawo usayizi omkhulu,**
a bigger size/	**omncane?**
in a smaller size?	oonaa:wo oosaayee:zee
	omkoo:loo, omŋ/aa:ne?
Do you have this	**Unayo eminye imibala?**
in any other	oonaa:yo emee:nye ee-
colours?	meebaa:laa?
That's a shame!	**Kuyadabukisa!**
	kooyaadaaboogee:saa!
It's too short	**Kufushane kakhulu**
	koofooshaa:ne kaakoo:loo
It's too long	**Kude kakhulu**
	koo:de kaakoo:loo
It's too big	**Kukhulu kakhulu**
	kookoo:loo kaakoo:loo

It's too small	**Kuncane kakhulu**
	kooŋ/aa:ne kaakoo:loo
I'm just looking	**Ngiyabuka-nje**
	ngeeyaaboo:gaanje
I'll take it	**Ngiyokuthenga.**
	ngeeyogoote:ngaa

Clothes (articles)

belt	**ibhande**	eebaa:nde
blouse	**ibhulawuzi**	eeboolaawoo:zee
bra	**ubra**	oo:braa
coat	**ijazi**	eejaa:zee
dress	**ilokwe**	eelo:gwe
dressing gown	**igawuni**	eegaawoo:nee
fleece	**isikhumba semvu**	eeskoo:mbaa se:mvoo

63

ukotini	ookotee:nee	cotton
usilika	ooseelee:kaa	silk
uleyisi	ooleyee:see	lace
uvolo	oovo:lo	wool

gloves	**amagilavu**	aamaageelaa:voo
hat	**isigqoko**	ees!g̣o:go
jacket	**ibhantshi**	eebaa:nchee
nightdress	**ilokwe lokulala**	eelo:gwe
		logoolaa:laa
panties	**isikhindi**	eeskee:ndee
	sangaphansi	saangaapaa:ntsee
pyjamas	**amaphijama**	aamaapeejaa:maa
raincoat	**ijazi lemvula**	eejaa:zee
		lemvoo:laa
sandals	**amasandali**	aamaasanda:lee
scarf (silk)	**isikhafu**	eeskaa:foo
	sikasilika	seegaaseelee:kaa
scarf (woollen)	**isikhafu**	eeskaa:foo
	sikavolo	seegaavo:lo
shirt	**ihembe**	eehe:mbe
shoes	**izicathulo**	eezee/ʔatoo:lo
shorts	**isikhindi**	eeskee:ndee
skirt	**isiketi**	eeske:tee
slippers	**amasiliphazi**	aamaasleepaa:zee
socks	**amasokisi**	aamaasogee:see
suit (woman's)	**isudi**	eesoo:dee
	lowesifazane	lowesfaazaa:ne
suit (man's)	**isudi**	eesoo:dee
swimsuit	**izingubo**	eezeengoo:bo
	zokubhukuda	zogooboogoo:daa

tights	**amathayithi**	aamaataayee:tee
t-shirt	**isikibha**	eeskee:baa
tracksuit	**itreksudi**	eetreksoo:dee
trainers	**amateki**	aamaate:kee
trousers	**ibhulukwe**	eebooloo:gwe
zip	**uziphu**	oozee:poo

Maps and guides

Do you have a map of the town?	**Unalo ibalazwe ledolobha?** oonaa:lo eebaalaa:zwe ledolo:baa?
Do you have a map of the region?	**Unalo ibalazwe lesifunda?** oonaa:lo eebaalaa:zwe lesfoo:ndaa?
Can you show me where ... is on the map?	**Ungangikhombisa ... ebalazweni?** oongaangeekombee:-saa ... ebaalaazwe:nee?
Do you have a detailed map of the area?	**Unalo ibalazwe elibonisa zonke izindawo?** oonaa:lo eebaalaa:zwe eleebonee:saa zo:nke eezeendaa:wo?
Where can I buy an English newspaper?	**Ngingalithengaphi iphephandaba lesiNgisi?** ngeengaaleetengaa:pee eepepaandaa:baa le-seengee:see?

> **Paying** (p 87) > **Numbers** (p 108)

| Do you have any English newspapers? | **Unawo amaphephandaba esiNgisi?** |
| | oonaa:wo aamaapepaandaa:-baa eseengee:see? |

Post office

Post offices are usually open from 8.30 am to 4.30 pm on weekdays, and from 8 am till 12 pm on Saturdays. There are smaller post points in pharmacies and supermarkets which may even be open on a Sunday.

Is there a post office near here?	**Likhona iposi eliseduze nalapha?**
	leeko:naa eepo:see eleesedoo:-ze naalaa:paa?
When is it open?	**Livulwa nini?**
	leevoo:lwaa nee:nee?
Which counter is it for stamps?	**Ngingazithola kuliphi ikhawunta izitembu?**
	ngeengaazeeto:laa koolee:pee eekaawoo:ntaa eezeete:mboo?
Which counter is it for parcels?	**Amaphasela alandwa kuliphi ikhawunta?**
	aamaapaase:laa aalaa:ndwaa koolee:pee eekaawoo:ntaa?
Three stamps for postcards to Great Britain	**Izitembu ezintathu zamaphosikadi aya eNgilandi**
	eezeete:mboo ezeentaa:too zaamaaposeekaa:dee aa:yaa engeela:ndee

iposi	**eepo:see**	post office
izitembu	**eezeete:mboo**	stamps

Two stamps for postcards to Canada
Izitembu ezimbili zamaphosikadi aya eKhanada
eezeete:mboo ezeembee:lee zaamaaposeekaa:dee aa:yaa ekana:daa

Four stamps for postcards to Australia
Izitembu ezine zamaphosikhadi aya e-Australia
eezeete:mboo ezee:ne zaamaaposeekaa:dee aa:yaa eaustralia

How much is it to send this parcel?
Yimalini ukuthumela leli phasela?
yeemaalee:nee oogootoome:laa le:lee paase:laa?

Photos

A film for this camera, please
Ngicela ifilimu yale khamera
ngee/ʔe:laa eefeelee:moo yaa:le kame:raa

Do you have batteries for this camera?
Unawo amabhethri ale khamera?
oonaa:wo aamaabe:tree aa:le kame:raa?

Do you have a memory card for this digital camera?
Unayo i-memory card yale khamera eyi-digital?
oonaa:yo eememory card yaa:le kame:raa eyeedigital?

67

Leisure

Sightseeing and tourist office
. . . .

Tourism information offices are scattered throughout
South Africa. The official local tourism information
sign is the letter 'I' on a brown road sign. Tourism
offices provide maps and brochures containing
information on tourist attractions, accommodation,
restaurants and local events.

Leisure

Where is the tourist office?	**Likuphi ihhovisi lezihambi?** leegoo:pee eehovee:see lezeehaa:mbee?
What is there to visit in the area?	**Yiziphi izindawo esingazivakashela?** yeezee:pee eezeendaa:wo eseengaazeevaagaashe:laa?
What is there to visit in the area in ... hours?	**Yiziphi izindawo esingazivakashela phakathi kwamahora angu-... ?** yeezee:pee eezeendaa:wo eseengaazeevaagaashe:laa paagaa:tee kwaamaaho:raa aangoo...?

Do you have any leaflets?	**Unawo amapheshana?**
	oonaa:wo aamaapeshaa:naa?
Are there any excursions?	**Lukhona uhambo lokungcebeleka?**
	looko:naa oohaa:mbo logoo-ŋ/gebele:gaa?
We'd like to go to...	**Singathanda ukuya e...**
	seengaataa:ndaa ogooo:yaa e...
How much does it cost to get in?	**Yimalini ukungena?**
	yeemaalee:nee oogoonge:naa?
Are there any reductions for...?	**Zikhona izaphulelo...?**
	zeeko:naa ezaapoole:lo...?
children	**zabantwana, zezingane**
	zaabaantwaa:naa, zezeengaa:ne
students	**zezitshudeni**
	zezeechoode:nee
the unemployed	**zabangasebenzi**
	zaabaangaasebe:ndzee
senior citizens	**zezakhamuzi ezindala**
	zeezaakaamoo:zee ezeendaa:laa

Entertainment

The local tourism office will have information on local events. You can also make use of the internet to find out about any happenings.

What is there to do in the evenings?	**Yini okuvame ukwenziwa kusihlwa?**
	yee:nee ogoovaa:me oogwendzee:waa koosee:ɬwaa?

69

Do you have a list of events for this month?	**Unalo uhlu lwezinto ezenziwa kule nyanga?**
	oonaa:lo oo:ɬoo lwezee:nto ezendzee:waa koo:le nyaa:ngaa?
Is there anything for children to do?	**Ikhona imidlalo yezingane?**
	eeko:naa eemeeɬaa:lo yezeengaa:ne?

Leisure/interests

•••••••••••••••••••••••••••••••••••••

Where can I/we...?	**Nginga...phi?, Singa... phi?***
	ngeengaa...pee?, seengaa... pee?
go fishing	**...doba...**
	...do:baa...
go riding	**...gibela... ihhashi**
	...geebe:laa... eehaa:shee
Are there any good (sandy) beaches near here?	**Akhona amabhishi amahle (anesihlabathi esiningi) eduze?**
	aako:naa aamaabee:shee aamaa:ɬe (aanesɬaabaa:tee eseenee:ngee) edoo:ze?
Is there a swimming pool?	**Likhona idamu lokubhukuda?**
	leeko:naa eedaa:moo logooboogoo:daa?

Safari/game reserves

•••••••••••••••••••••••••••••••••••••

South Africa has world-renowned, well-stocked game parks that are certainly one of the country's main attractions. The game parks are both national and

70

private and are located across the country. Accommodation varies from the ultra-luxurious to very affordable camping. Some game parks can be accessed for day trips.

baboon	imfene	eemfe:ne
beetle	ibhungane	eeboongaa:ne
bird	inyoni	eenyo:nee
black rhino	ubhejane	oobejaa:ne
blue crane	indwa	ee:ndwaa
buffalo	inyathi	eenyaa:tee
butterfly	uvemvane	oovemvaa:ne
bush buck	unkonka	oonko:nkaa
bush-pig	ingulube yasendle	eengooloo:be yaase:nɮe
chameleon	unwabu	oonwaa:boo
cheetah	ingulule	eengooloo:le
crested crane	unohemu	oonohe:moo
crocodile	ingwenya	eengwe:nyaa
duiker	impunzi	eempoo:ndzee
eland	impofu	eempo:foo
elephant	indlovu	eenɮo:voo
giraffe	indlulamithi	eenɮoolaamee:tee
hartebeest	indluzele	eenɮooze:le
hippo	imvubu	eemvoo:boo
hyena	impisi	eempee:see
jackal	ujakalasi	oojaagaalaa:see
kudu	umgankla	oomgaa:nklaa
impala	impala	eempaa:laa
leopard	ingwe	ee:ngwe
lion	ibhubesi	eeboobe:see

mamba	imamba	eemaa:mbaa
monkey	inkawu	eenkaa:woo
mosquito	umiyane	oomeeyaa:ne
ostrich	intshe	ee:nche
puffadder	ibululu	eebooloo:loo
python	inhlwathi	eenɬwaa:tee
reedbuck	inhlangu	eenɬaa:ngoo
scorpion	ufezela	oofeze:laa
snake	inyoka	eenyo:gaa
spider	isicabucabu	ees/ˀaaboo/ˀaa:boo
springbuck	insephe	eentse:pe
tortoise	ufudu	oofoo:doo
white rhino	umkhombe	oomko:mbe
warthog	intibane	eenteebaa:ne
wildebeest/gnu	inkonkoni	eenkonko:nee

Music

Are there any good concerts on?	**Akhona amakhonsathi amahle adlalayo?** aako:naa aamaakontsaa:tee aamaa:ɬe aaƚaalaa:yo?
Where can I get tickets for the concert?	**Ngingawathengaphi amathikithi ekhonsathi?** ngeengaawaatengaa:pee aamaateegee:tee ekontsaa:tee?
Where can we hear some classical music?	**Singawulalelaphi umculo wekilasiki?** seengaawoolaalelaa:pee oom/ˀoo:lo wekeelasee:kee?

72

Where can we hear some jazz?

Singayilalelaphi ijezi?
seengaayeelaalelaa:pee eeje:zee?

Cinema

. . . .

ifilimu enenkumusho eefeelee:moo enenkoomoo:sho	subtitled
umbukiso oomboogee:so	performance
ngolimi lwayo ngolee:mee lwaa:yo	in the original language (i.e. not dubbed)

What's on at the cinema?	**Yimaphi amafilimu adlalwa ebhayisikobho?** yeemaa:pee aamaafeelee:moo aƙaa:lwaa ebaayeeseeko:bo?
When does the film start/finish?	**Ifilimu iqala, iphela ngasikhathi sini?** eefeelee:moo ee!ʔaa:laa, eepe:laa ngaaskaa:tee see:nee?
How much are the tickets?	**Amalini amathikithi?** aamaalee:nee aamaateegee:tee?
I'd like ... tickets, please	**Ngingacela amathikithi angu-...** ngeengaa/ʔe:laa aamaateegee:tee aangoo...

73

Theatre/opera

umdlalo oomʒaa:lo	play
umbukiso oomboogee:so	performance
ezihlalweni eziphambi kwesiteji ethiyetha ezee4aalwe:nee ezeepaa:mbee kweste:jee etheeye:taa	in the stalls
ezihlalweni eziphezulu ethiyetha ezee4aalwe:nee ezeepezoo:loo etheeye:taa	in the circle
isihlalo ees4aa:lo	seat
ikhefu eeke:foo	interval

What is on at the opera?	**Kudlalani kwi-ophera?** kooʒaalaa:nee kweeope:raa?
What is on at the theatre?	**Kudlalani ethiyetha?** kooʒaalaa:nee etheeye:taa?
What prices are the tickets?	**Amalini amathikithi?** aamaalee:nee aamaateegee:tee?
I'd like ... tickets	**Ngicela amathikithi angu-...** ngee/ʔe:laa aamaateegee:tee aangoo...
for tonight	**anamhlanje ebusuku** aanaam4aa:nje eboosoo:goo
for tomorrow night	**akusasa ebusuku** aagoosaa:saa eboosoo:goo
for 5th August	**angomhla ka-5 ku-Agasti** aango:m4aa kaa5 kooaagaa:stee

When does the performance begin?	**Umbukiso uqala ngasikhathi sini?** oomboogee:so oo!ʔaa:laa ngaaskaa:tee see:nee?	
When does the performance end?	**Umbukiso uphela ngasikhathi sini?** oomboogee:so oope:laa ngaaskaa:tee see:nee?	

Television

. . . .

irimothi ereemo:tee	remote control
umdlalo owuchungechunge oomӄaa:lo owoo/hoonge/hoo:nge	soap
i-DVD eedvd	DVD
isidlali ma-DVD eesӄaa:lee maadvd	DVD player
izindaba eezeendaa:baa	news
-vula* -voo:laa	to switch on
-cima* -/ʔee:maa	to switch off
izinhlelo eezeenɬe:lo	programme
amakhathuni aamaakaatoo:nee	cartoons

Where is the television?	**I-TV ikuphi?** eetv eegoo:pee?	
How do you switch it on?	**Ngiyivula kanjani?** ngeeyeevoo:laa kaanjaa:nee?	

> **Making friends** (p 22)

What is on television?	**Kukhonjiswani kwi-TV?**
	kookonjeeswaa:nee kweetv?
When is the news?	**Izindaba zingasikhathi sini?**
	eezeendaa:baa zeengaaskaa:tee see:nee?

Sport

Where can I/ we...?	**Nginga...phi?, Singa... phi?***
	ngeengaa...pee?, seengaa...pee?
Where can I/ we play tennis?	**Ngingalidlalaphi, Singalidlalaphi ithenisi?**
	ngeengaaleeȝaalaa:pee, seengaaleeȝaalaa:pee eetenee:see?
Where can I/ we play golf?	**Ngingalidlalaphi, Singalidlalaphi igalofu?**
	ngeengaaleeȝaalaa:pee, seengaaleeȝaalaa:pee eegaalo:foo?
Where can I/we go swimming?	**Ngingabhukudaphi, Singabhukudaphi?**
	ngeengaaboogoodaa:pee, seengaaboogoodaa:pee?
Where can I/ we go jogging?	**Ngingagijimaphi, Singagijimaphi?**
	ngeengaageejeemaa:pee, seengaageejeemaa:pee?
How much is it per hour?	**Yimalini ngehora?**
	yeemaalee:nee ngeho:raa?

Do you have to be a member?	**Kufanele ube yilunga?**
	koofaane:le oobe yeeloo:ngaa?
Can we hire rackets?	**Singawaqasha amarakethi?**
	seengaawaa!?aa:shaa aamaarake:tee?
Can we hire golf clubs?	**Singaziqasha izinduku zegalofu?**
	seengaazee!?aa:shaa eezeendoo:goo zegaloo:foo?
Where can I/ we get tickets?	**Ngingawatholaphi, Singawatholaphi amathikithi?**
	ngeengaawaatolaa:pee, seengaawaatolaa:pee aamaateegee:tee?
What sports do you play?	**Yimiphi imidlalo oyidlalayo?**
	yeemee:pee eemeeɮaa:lo oyeeɮaalaa:yo?

Amathikithi omdlalo aphelile.	There are no tickets left for the game.
aamaateegee:tee omɮaa:- lo aapelee:le.	

Walking

Are there any guided walks?	**Ingabe lukhona uhambo ngezinyawo oluneziqondiso?**
	eengaa:be looko:naa oohaa:mbo ngezeenyaa:wo oloonezee!?ondee:so?

Do you have a guide to local walks?	**Unalo yini ibhuku elikhombisa uhambo ngezinyawo endaweni?**
	oonaa:lo yee:nee eeboo:goo eleekombee:saa oohaa:mbo ngezeenyaa:wo endaawe:nee?
Do you know any good walks?	**Zikhona izindawo ezinhle ezihanjwa ngezinyawo?**
	zeeko:naa eezeendaa:wo ezee:n⁴e ezeehaa:njwaa ngezeenyaa:wo?
How many kilometres is the walk?	**Uhambo lungathatha amakhilomitha amangaki?**
	oohaa:mbo loongaataataa:taa aamaakeelomee:taa aamaangaa:gee?
How long will it take?	**Luzothatha isikhathi esingakanani?**
	loozotaa:taa eeskaa:tee eseengaagaanaa:nee?
Is it very steep?	**Ingabe lunomqanso?**
	eengaa:be loonom!ʔaa:ntso?
We'd like to go climbing	**Singathanda ukuqombola izintaba**
	seengaataa:ndaa oogoo!ʔombo:laa eezeentaa:baa

> **Maps and guides** (p 65)

Communications

Telephone and mobile

The international dialling code for South Africa is
0027 plus the South African number that you require
without the first 0 of the area code. When you dial a
number in South Africa while in the country, you
must dial the area code before the actual number
even for local calls.

I'd like to make a phone call	**Ngingathanda ukushaya ucingo** ngeengaataa:ndaa oogooshaa:yaa oo/ʔee:ngo
Is there a pay phone?	**Ikhona indawo yokushaya ucingo?** eeko:naa eendaa:wo yogooshaa:yaa oo/ʔee:ngo?
A phonecard, please for ... South African Rand	**Ngicela ikhadi lokushaya ucingo lamarandi angu-...** ngee/ʔe:laa eekaa:dee logooshaa:yaa oo/ʔee:ngo laamaaraa:ndee angoo...
Do you have a mobile?	**Unaye umakhalekhukhwini?** oonaa:ye oomaakaalekoo-kwee:nee?

79

Communications

What's your mobile number?	**Ithini inombolo yakho kamakhalekhukhwini?**
	eetee:nee eenombo:lo yaa:ko kaamaakaalekookwee:nee?
Can I use your mobile?	**Ngingawusebenzisa umakhalekhukhwini wakho?**
	ngeengaawoosebendzee:saa oomaakaalekookwee:nee waa:ko?
My mobile number is...	**Inombolo yami kamakhalekhukhwini ithi...**
	eenombo:lo yaa:mee kaamaakaalekookwee:nee ee:tee...
Mnumzane Madonsela, please	**Ngicela ukukhuluma noMnumzane Madonsela**
	ngee/ʔe:laa oogookooloo:maa nomnoomzaa:ne maadontse:laa
Extension...	**Ku-extension...**
	kooextension...

FACE TO FACE

A **Sawubona?**
saawoobo:naa?
Hello

B **Yebo, sawubona. Ngicela ukukhuluma no...**
ye:bo, saawoobo:naa. ngee/ʔe:laa oogookooloo:maa no...
Hello. I'd like to speak to... , please

80

A Ngubani okhulumayo?
ngoobaa:nee okooloomaa:yo?
Who's calling?

B Ngu...
ngoo...
This is...

A Awubambe kancane...
aawoobaa:mbe kaaŋ/aa:ne...
Just a moment...

Can I speak to...?	**Ngicela ukukhuluma no...?** ngee/ˀe:laa oogookooloo:maa no...?
It's (your name)	**Ngu...** ngoo...
How do I get an outside line?	**Ngingaphumela kanjani ngaphandle kwehhotela?** ngeengaapoome:laa kaanjaa:nee ngaapaa:nʒe kwehote:laa?
I'll call back later	**Ngizobuye ngishaye** ngeezoboo:ye ngeeshaa:ye
I'll call back tomorrow	**Ngizokushayela kusasa** ngeezogooshaaye:laa koosaa:saa

YOU MAY HEAR...

Ngiyakwedlulisela. ngeeyaagweʒooleese:laa	I'm putting you through
Lumatasatasa loomaataasaataa:saa	It's engaged

Telephone and mobile

81

Ngicela uzame kamuva ngee/ʔe:laa oozaa:me kaamoo:vaa	Please try later
Ufuna ukushiya umyalezo? oofoo:naa oogooshee:yaa oomyaale:zo?	Do you want to leave a message?
Ngicela ushiye umyalezo emva kwethoni ngee/ʔe:laa ooshee:ye oomyaale:zo e:mvaa kweto:nee	Please leave a message after the tone
Ngicela ucime umakhalekhukhwini wakho ngee/ʔe:laa oo/ʔee:me oomaakaalekookwee:nee waa:ko	Please turn your mobile off

Text messaging
. . . .

I will text/ SMS you	**Ngizokuthumela i-SMS** ngeezogootoome:laa eesms
Can you text/ SMS me?	**Ungangithumela i-SMS?** oongaangeetoome:laa eesms?

E-mail
. . . .

New message	**Umyalezo omusha** oomyaale:zo omoo:shaa
To	**Oya ku... *** o:yaa koo...

82

From	**Ovela ku...** *
	ove:laa koo...
Subject	**Isihloko**
	ees‡o:go
Attachment	**Okufakiwe**
	ogoofaagee:we
Send	**Thumela**
	toome:laa
Do you have an e-mail address?	**Unalo ikheli le-e-mail?**
	oonaa:lo eeke:lee le-email?
What's your e-mail address?	**Lithini ikheli lakho le-e-mail?**
	leetee:nee eeke:lee laa:ko le-email?
How do you spell it?	**Lipelwa kanjani?**
	leepe:lwaa kaanjaa:nee?
All one word	**Yigama elilodwa**
	yeegaa:maa eleelo:dwaa
All lower case	**Lingonobumba abancane kuphela**
	leengonoboo:mbaa aabaa-ŋ/aa:ne koope:laa
My e-mail address is...	**Ikheli lami le-e-mail lithi...**
	eeke:lee laa:mee le-email lee:tee...
caroline.smith@ (co. name).co.za	**caroline.smith@abcdefg.co.za**
	caroline.smith@abcdefg.co.za
Can I send an e-mail?	**Ngingakuthumelela i-e-mail?**
	ngeengaakootoomele:laa ee-email?
Did you get my e-mail?	**Uyitholile i-e-mail yami?**
	ooyeetolee:le ee-email yaa:mee?

E-mail

Internet

ekhaya ekaa:yaa	home
igama lomsebenzisi eegaa:maa lomsebendzee:see	username
injini yokucinga eenjee:nee yogoo/ʔee:ngaa	search engine
iphasiwedi eepaaseewe:dee	password
thintana nathi teentaa:naa naa:tee	contact us
buyela kwimenu booye:laa kweemenu	back to menu

Are there any internet cafés here?

Zikhona yini izikhungo ze-inthanethi lapha?
zeeko:naa yee:nee eezeekoo:ngo ze-eentane:tee laa:paa?

How much is it to log on for an hour?

Yimalini ukusebenzisa i-inthanethi ngehora?
yeemaalee:nee oogoosebendzee:saa ee-eentane:tee ngeho:raa?

I can't log on

Angikwazi ukungena kwi-inthanethi
aangeegwaa:zee oogoonge:naa kwee-eentane:tee

84

Communications

Fax

● ●

addressing a fax	**ukubhala ikheli esikhahlamezini** oogoobaa:laa eeke:lee eskaaɬaamezee:nee
To/From	**Esiya ku..., Esivela ku...** * esee:yaa koo..., eseeve:laa koo...
Re:	**Mayelana na..., ne..., no...** * maayelaa:naa naa..., ne..., no...
Number of pages	**Isibalo samakhasi** eesbaa:lo saamaakaa:see
Please find attached...	**Ngicela ubheke okufakiwe...** ngee/ʔe:laa oobe:ge ogoofaagee:we...
Do you have a fax?	**Unaso isikhahlamezi?** oonaa:so eeskaaɬaame:zee?
I want to send a fax	**Ngifuna ukuthumela isikhahlamezi** ngeefoo:naa oogootoome:laa eeskaaɬaame:zee
What is your fax number?	**Ithini inombolo yakho yesikhahlamezi?** eetee:nee eenombo:lo yaa:ko yeskaaɬaame:zee?
My fax number is...	**Inombolo yami yesikhahlamezi ithi...** eenombo:lo yaa:mee yeskaaɬaame:zee ee:tee...

Practicalities

Money

Banking hours vary slightly, but are generally from 9 am to 3.30 pm from Monday to Friday, and from 8.30 am to 11.30 am on Saturday. Some banks are even open on a Sunday till 1.00 pm. Banks are generally closed on Public Holidays. Readily-accessible 24-hour ATMs are found in shopping malls, at petrol stations, airports, in some hotel lobbies and even in some hospitals. Major credit cards are widely accepted, but cannot be used to pay for fuel at petrol stations.

i-ATM eeatm	cash dispenser/ATM
ukukhishwa kwemali oogookee:shwaa kwemaa:lee	cash withdrawal

Where can I change some money?	**Ngingayishintshaphi imali?** ngeengaayeesheenchaa:pee eemaa:lee?
I want to change these traveller's cheques	**Ngifuna ukushintsha la masheke ezihambi** ngeefoo:naa oogooshee:nchaa laa maashe:ge ezeehaa:mbee

When does the bank open?	Ibhange livula ngasikhathi sini?
	eebaa:nge leevoo:laa ngaaskaa:tee see:nee?
When does the bank close?	Ibhange livala ngasikhathi sini?
	eebaa:nge leevaa:laa ngaaskaa:tee see:nee?
Can I pay with dollars?	Ngingakhokha ngamadola?
	ngeengaako:kaa ngaamaado:laa?
Can I use my credit card with this cash machine?	Ngingayisebenzisa i-credit card lami kule ATM?
	ngeengaayeesebendzee:saa eecredit card yaa:mee koo:le atm?
Do you have any change?	Unawo ushintshi?
	oonaa:wo ooshee:nchee?

Paying

i-akhawunti	bill (restaurant/hotel)
eeakaawoo:ntee	
i-invoyisi	invoice
ee-eenvoyee:see	
lapho kukhokhwa khona	cash desk/till
laa:po kooko:kwaa ko:naa	

How much is it?	Yimalini?
	yeemaalee:nee?
How much will it be?	Kuzoba malini?
	koozo:baa maalee:nee?
Can I pay by credit card?	Ngingakhokha nge-credit card?
	ngeengaako:kaa ngecredit card?

Can I pay by cheque?	**Ngingakhokha ngesheke?** ngeengaako:kaa ngeshe:ge?
Put it on my bill (hotel)	**Kufake kwi-akhawunti yami** koofaa:ke kweeakaawoo:ntee yaa:mee
The bill, please (restaurant)	**Ngicela i-akhawunti** ngee/ʔe:laa eeakaawoo:ntee
Where do I pay?	**Ngikhokha kuphi?** ngeeko:kaa koo:pee?
Do you take credit cards?	**Niyawathatha ama-credit card?** neeyaawaataa:taa aamaacredit card?
Is service included?	**Ingabe nesevisi ihlanganisiwe?** eengaa:be nesevee:see eeɬaangaaneesee:we?
Could you give me a receipt, please?	**Ngicela irisidi.** ngee/ʔe:laa eereesee:dee.
Do I pay in advance?	**Kufanele ngikhokhe kusengaphambili?** koofaane:le ngeeko:ke koosengaapaambee:lee?
I'm sorry	**Ngiyaxolisa** ngeeyaa//ʔolee:saa
I've nothing smaller (change)	**Anginashintshi** aangeenaashee:nchee

Luggage

My luggage hasn't arrived yet	**Umthwalo wami awakafiki** oomtwaa:lo waa:mee aa-waagaafee:gee

indawo yokulanda umthwalo eendaa:wo yogoolaa:ndaa oomtwaa:lo	baggage reclaim
umthwalo oshiyiwe oomtwaa:loo osheeyee:we	left luggage
inqola yomthwalo eeŋ!o:laa yomtwaa:lo	luggage trolley

My suitcase has been damaged on the flight	**Isutikesi lami lilinyazwe ebhanoyini** eesooteeke:see laa:mee leeleenyaa:zwe ebaanoyee:nee

Repairs

. . . .

okhanda izicathulo okaa:ndaa eezee?/aatoo:lo	shoe repairer
ukhanda lapho ulindile ookaa:ndaa laa:po ooleendee:le	repairs while you wait

This is broken	**Lokhu kuphukile** lo:koo koopoogee:le
Where can I get this repaired?	**Ngingakukhandisa kuphi lokhu?** ngeengaagookaandee:saa koo:pee lo:koo?
Can you repair these shoes?	**Ungazikhanda lezi zicathulo?** oongaazeekaa:ndaa le:zee zee/?aatoo:lo?

| Can you repair my watch? | **Ungalikhanda leli washi?** |
| | oongaaleekaa:ndaa le:lee waa:shee? |

Laundry

ilondolo eelondo:lo	dry-cleaner's/ launderette
impuphu yokuwasha eempoo:poo yogoowaa:shaa	washing powder

| Where can I do some washing? | **Ngingaziwashaphi izingubo?** ngeengaazeewaashaa:pee eezeengoo:bo? |
| Is there a launderette/ dry-cleaner's near here? | **Ikhona ilondolo eseduze?** eeko:naa eelondo:lo esedoo:ze? |

Complaints

This doesn't work	**Le nto ayisebenzi** le nto aayeesebe:ndzee
It's dirty	**Kungcolile** kooŋ/golee:le
The ... doesn't/ don't work	**Negative + -sebenzi *** ...sebe:ndzee
light	**isibani** eesbaa:nee

lock	**ingidi**
	eengee:dee
heating	**ukufudumeza**
	oogoofoodoome:zaa
air conditioning	**ukupholiswa**
	nokufudunyezwa komoya
	oogoopolee:swaa
	nogoofoodoonye:zwaa
	komo:yaa
It's broken	**Kuphukile**
	koopoogee:le
I want a refund	**Ngifuna imbuyiselo**
	ngeefoo:naa eembooyeese:lo

Problems

. . . .

Can you help me?	**Ungangisiza?**
	oongaangeesee:zaa?
I speak very little Zulu	**Ngisazi kancane kakhulu isiZulu**
	ngeesaa:zee kaaŋ/aa:ne kakoo:loo eeseezoo:loo
Does anyone here speak English?	**Ukhona umuntu lapha okhuluma isiNgisi?**
	ooko:naa oomoo:ntoo laa:paa okooloo:maa eeseenge:see?
I would like to speak to whoever is in charge	**Ngingathanda ukukhuluma nomphathi**
	ngeengaataa:ndaa oogookooloo:maa nompaa:tee
I'm lost	**Ngidukile**
	ngeedoogee:le

How do I get to...?	**Ngingafika kanjani e...?**
	ngeengaafee:gaa kaanjaa:nee e...?
I missed my train	**Ngishiywe yisitimela**
	ngeeshee:ywe yeesteeme:laa
I missed my plane	**Ngishiywe yibhanoyi**
	ngeeshee:ywe yeebaano:yee
I missed my connection	**Ngishiywe yintilasipoti**
	ngeeshee:ywe yeenteelaaseepo:tee
The coach has left without me	**Ngishiywe yibhasi**
	ngeeshee:ywe yeebaa:see
I have lost my purse	**Ngilahlekelwe yisikhwama sami semali**
	ngeelaa∤ege:lwe yeeskwaa:maa saa:mee semaa:lee
I need to get to...	**Kufanele ngiye e...**
	koofaane:le ngee:ye e...
Leave me alone!	**Hlukana nami!**
	∤oogaa:naa naa:mee!
Go away!	**Hamba!**
	haa:mbaa!

Emergencies

The nationwide emergency number for the police is 10111 and 10177 for the ambulance service.

Help!	**Ngisize!**
	ngeesee:ze!
Fire!	**Ngumlilo!**
	ngoomlee:lo!

Can you help me?	Ungangisiza?
	oongaangeesee:zaa?
There has been an accident	Kuvele ingozi
	koove:le eengo:zee
Someone has been injured	Umuntu ulimele
	oomoo:ntoo ooleeme:le
She/he has been knocked down by a car	Ushayiswe ngemoto
	ooshaayee:swe ngemo:to
Please call the police	Ngicela ubize amaphoyisa
	ngee/ʔe:laa oobee:ze aamaapoyee:saa
Please call an ambulance	Ngicela ubize i-ambhulense
	ogee/ʔe:laa oobee:ze eeamboole:ntse

amaphoyisa aamaapoyee:saa	police
i-ambhulense eeamboole:ntse	ambulance
isicimamlilo ees/ʔeemaamlee:lo	fire brigade
isiteshi samaphoyisa eeste:shee saamaapoyee:saa	police station
umnyango wezingozi nezimo eziphuthumayo oomnyaa:ngo wezeengo:zee nezee:mo ezeepootoomaa:yo	accident and emergency unit

Emergencies

Where is the police station?	Sikuphi isiteshi samaphoyisa?
	seegoo:pee eeste:shee saamaapoyee:saa?
I want to report a theft	Ngifuna ukubika ukweba
	ngeefoo:naa oogoobee:gaa oogwe:baa
I've been robbed	Ngiphangiwe
	ngeepaangee:we
I've been raped	Ngidlwenguliwe
	ngeeʒwengoolee:we
I want to speak to a policewoman	Ngifuna ukukhuluma nephoyisa lesifazane
	ngeefoo:naa oogookooloo:maa nepoyee:saa lesfaazaa:ne
Someone has stolen my handbag	Isikhwama sami sintshontshiwe
	eeskwaa:maa saa:mee seenchonchee:we
Someone has stolen my money	Imali yami intshontshiwe
	eemaa:lee yaa:mee eenchonchee:we
My car has been broken into	Imoto yami igqekeziwe
	eemo:to yaa:mee ee!ġegezee:we
My car has been stolen	Imoto yami intshontshiwe
	eemo:to yaa:mee eenchonchee:we
I need to make a telephone call	Ngifuna ukushaya ucingo
	ngeefoo:naa oogooshaa:yaa oo/ˀee:ngo
I need a report for my insurance	Ngidinga umbiko ngomshuwalense wami
	ngeedee:ngaa oombee:go ngomshoowaale:ntse waa:mee

I didn't know the speed limit	Bengingalazi ijubane elibekiwe
	bengeengaalaa:zee eejoobaa:ne eleebegee:we
How much is the fine?	Yimalini inhlawulo?
	yeemaalee:nee een4aawoo:lo?
Where do I pay it?	Ngiyikhokhephi?
	ngeeyeekoke:pee?
Do I have to pay it straight away?	Kufanele ngiyikhokhe ngokushesha?
	koofaane:le ngeeyeeko:ke ngogooshe:shaa?
I'm very sorry, officer	Ngiyaxolisa kakhulu, sikhulu
	ngeeyaa//ʔolee:saa kaakoo:loo, seekoo:loo

YOU MAY HEAR...

Udlule erobhothini elibomvu	You went through a red light
ooʒoo:le erobotee:nee eleebo:mvoo	
Awuzange ulinde	You didn't give way
aawoozaa:nge oolee:nde	

Emergencies

Health

Pharmacy

ikhemisi eekemee:see	pharmacy/chemist's
ikhemisi elivulwe ebusuku eekemee:see eleevoo:lwe eeboosoo:goo	after-hours chemist

Can you give me something for...?	**Unganginika umuthi...?** oongaangeenee:gaa oomoo:tee...
a headache	**wekhanda** wekaa:ndaa
car sickness	**wokungazizwa kahle emotweni** wogoongaazee:zwaa kaa:ɬe emotwe:nee
flu	**wemfuluwenza** wemfooloowe:ndzaa
diarrhoea	**wohudo** wohoo:do
sunburn	**wokushiswa yilanga** wogooshee:swaa yeelaa:ngaa
Is it safe for children?	**Uphephile kubantwana?** oopepee:le koobaantwaa:naa?

| How much should I give him/her? | **Kufanele ngimphuzise ongakanani?** |
| | koofaane:le ngeempoozee:se ongaagaanaa:nee? |

Wuphuze kathathu ngosuku ngaphambi kokudla woopoo:ze kaataa:too ngosoo:goo ngaapaa:mbee kogoo:ʒaa	Take it three times a day before meals
Wuphuze kathathu ngosuku uma udla woopoo:ze kaataa:too ngosoo:goo oo:maa oo:ʒaa	Take it three times a day with meals
Wuphuze kathathu ngosuku emva kokudla woopoo:ze kaataa:too ngosoo:goo e:mvaa kogoo:ʒaa	Take it three times a day after meals

Doctor

| I need a doctor | **Ngidinga udokotela** ngeedee:ngaa oodogote:laa |
| My son is ill | **Indodana yami iyagula** eendodaa:naa yaa:mee eeyaagoo:laa |

| isibhedlela eesbeʒe:laa | hospital |
| umnyango wezingozi nezimo eziphuthumayo oomnyaa:ngo wezeengo:zee nezee:mo ezeepootoomaa:yo | accident and emergency unit |

A **Angizizwa kahle.**
aangeezee:zwaa kaa:ɬe
I feel ill.

B **Uphethwe yimfiva?**
oope:twe yeemfee:vaa?
Do you have a temperature?

A **Cha, kubuhlungu lapha.**
/haa, koobooɬoo:ngoo laa:paa.
No, I have a pain here.

My daughter is ill	**Indodakazi yami iyagula** eendodagaa:zee yaa:mee eeyaagoo:laa
I'm diabetic	**Ngiphethwe yisifo sikashukela** ngeepe:twe yeesee:fo seegashooge:laa
I'm pregnant	**Ngikhulelwe** ngeekoole:lwe
I'm on the pill	**Ngisebenzisa iphilisi lokuvimbela inzalo** ngeesebendzee:saa eepeelee:see logooveembe:laa eendzaa:lo

98

I'm allergic to penicillin	**Angizwani nephenisilini**
	angeezwaa:nee nepeneeseelee:nee
Will she/he have to go to hospital?	**Kufanele aye esibhedlela?**
	koofaane:le aa:ye esbeʒe:laa?
Will I have to pay?	**Kufanele ngikhokhe?**
	koofaane:le ngeeko:ke?
How much will it cost?	**Kuzoba malini?**
	koozo:baa maalee:nee?
I need a receipt for the insurance	**Umshuwalense udinga irisidi**
	oomshoowaale:ntse oo-dee:ngaa eereesee:dee

YOU MAY HEAR...

Kufanele uye esibhedlela koofaane:le oo:ye esbeʒe:laa	You will have to go to hospital
Akukubi aagoogoo:bee	It's not serious

Dentist

I need to see a dentist	**Kufanele ngiye kudokotela wamazinyo**
	koofaane:le ngee:ye koodogote:laa waamaazee:nyo
He/She has toothache	**Uphethwe yizinyo**
	oope:twe yeezee:nyo

> **Emergencies** (p 92)

Dentist

Can you do a temporary filling?	**Ungalivala imbobo okwesikhashana?**
	oongaaleevaa:laa eembo:bo ogweskaashaa:naa?
Can you give me something for the pain?	**Unganginika isibulala-zinhlungu?**
	oongaangeenee:gaa eesboolaalaazeen4oo:ngoo?
It hurts	**Kubuhlungu**
	kooboo4oo:ngoo
Can you repair my dentures?	**Ungawalungisa amazinyo ami okufakelwa?**
	oongaawaaloongee:saa aamaazee:nyo aa:mee ogoofaage:lwaa?
Do I have to pay?	**Kufanele ngikhokhe?**
	koofaane:le ngeeko:ke?
How much will it be?	**Kuzoba malini?**
	koozo:baa maalee:nee?

Health

Different types of travellers

Disabled travellers

What facilities do you have for disabled people?
Ninamalungiselelo mani abantu abakhubazekile?
neenaamaaloongeesele:lo maa:nee aabaa:ntoo aabaakoobaazegee:le?

Are there any toilets for the disabled?
Akhona yini amathoyilethi abantu abakhubazekile?
aako:naa yee:nee aamaatoyeele:tee aabaa:ntoo aabaakoobaazegee:le?

Do you have any bedrooms on the ground floor?
Ninawo yini amakamelo ngaphansi kwesitezi?
neenaa:wo yee:nee aamaakaame:lo ngaapaa:ntsee kweste:zee?

Is there a lift?
Ikhona ilifti?
eeko:naa eelee:ftee?

Where is the lift?
Ilifti ikuphi?
eelee:ftee eegoo:pee?

Do you have wheelchairs?
Ninazo izihlalo zabakhubazekile?
neenaa:zo eezee‡aa:lo zaabaakoobaazegee:le?

Can you visit ... in a wheelchair?	Ungaya e... ngesihlalo sabakhubazekile?
	oongaya:yaa e... nges4aa:lo saabaakoobaazege:le?
Do you have an induction loop?	Ninayo yini i-induction loop?
	neenaa:yo yee:nee ee-induction loop?
Is there a reduction for disabled people?	Bayasithola yini isaphulelo abakhubazekile?
	baayaaseeto:laa yee:nee eesaapoole:lo aabaakoobaazege:le?
Is there somewhere I can sit down?	Ikhona indawo lapho ngingahlala phansi khona?
	eeko:naa eendaa:wo laa:po ngeengaa4aa:laa paa:ntsee ko:naa?

With kids

A child's ticket	Ithikithi lomntwana
	eeteegee:tee lomntwaa:naa
He/She is ... years old	Uneminyaka engu-...
	oonemeenyaa:gaa engoo-...
Is there a reduction for children?	Abantwana bathola isaphulelo?
	aabaantwaa:naa baato:laa eesaapoole:lo?
Do you have a children's menu?	Ninako ukudla kwabantwana?
	neenaa:ko oogoo:ɮaa kwaabaantwaa:naa?

> **Hotel desk** (p 51)

Is it okay to take children?	Kuvumelekile ukuhamba nezingane? koovoomelegee:le oogoohaa:mbaa nezeengaa:ne?
Do you have a high chair?	Ninaso isihlalo sokudlisa umntwana? neenaa:so eesɬaa:lo sogooƚgee:saa oomntwaa:naa?
Do you have a cot?	Ninawo umbhede womntwana? neenaa:wo oombe:de womntwaa:naa?
I have two children	Nginabo abantwana ababili ngeenaa:bo aabaantwaa:naa aabaabee:lee
He/She is 10 years old	Uneminyaka engu-10 oonemeenyaa:gaa engoo10
Do you have any children?	Unabo abantwana? oonaa:bo aabaantwaa:naa?

Business
. . . .

I am...	Ngingu... ngeengoo...
Here's my card	Nanti ikhadi lami naa:ntee eekaa:dee laa:mee
I'm from the Smith company	Ngisebenzela inkampani yakwa-Smith ngeesebendze:laa eenkaampaa:nee yagwaasmith

> **Pharmacy** (p 96) > **Doctor** (p 97)

I'd like to arrange an appointment	**Ngingathanda ukuhlela isikhathi sokubonana** ngeengaataa:ndaa oogoo4e:laa eeskaa:tee sogoobonaa:naa
With Mr/Ms...	**NoMnumzane, noNkosikazi...** nomnoomzaa:ne, nonkoseegaa:zee...
Can we meet at a restaurant?	**Singahlangana esitolo sokudlela?** seengaa4aangaa:naa esto:lo sogoo4e:laa?
I will send a fax to confirm	**Ngizothumela isikhahlamezi ukuqinisekisa** ngeezotoome:laa eeskaa4aame:zee oogoo!?eeneesegee:saa
I'm staying at Hotel...	**Ngihlala ehhotela elithi...** ngee4aa:laa ehote:laa elee:tee...
How do I get to your office?	**Ngingafika kanjani ehhovisini lakho?** ngeengaafee:gaa kaanjaa:nee ehoveesee:nee laa:ko?
Here's some information about my company	**Nakhu ukwaziswa mayelana nenkampani yami** naa:koo oogwaazee:swaa mayelaa:naa nenkaampaa:nee yaa:mee
I have an appointment with... at... o'clock	**Ngifanele ngibonane no... ngo-...** ngeefaane:le ngeebonaa:ne no... ngo...

Delighted to meet you	Ngijabulela ukukwazi ngeejaaboole:laa oogoogwaa:zee
My Zulu isn't very good	IsiZulu sami asisihle kangako eeseezoo:loo saa:mee aaseesee:ɬe kaangaa:go
I would like some information about your company	Ngingathanda ukwaziswa mayelana nenkampani yakho ngeengaataa:ndaa oogwaazee:swaa maayelaa:naa nenkaampaa:nee yaa:ko
Can you photocopy this for me?	Ungangenzela ifothokhophi yale nto? oongaangendze:laa eefotoko:pee yaa:le nto?

| Kukhona ohlele ukubonana naye? kooko:naa oɬe:le oogoobonaa:naa naa:ye? | Do you have an appointment? |

Business

105

Reference

Alphabet

The Zulu alphabet is the same as the English. When a word is spelled aloud in Zulu, English spelling is used.

Measurements and quantities

1 lb = approx. 0.5 kilo 1 pint = approx. 0.5 litre

Liquids

1/2 litre...	**uhhafu welitha...**
	oohaa:foo welee:ta...
a litre of...	**ilitha la..., le..., lo...***
	eelee:ta laa..., le..., lo...
1/2 bottle of...	**uhhafu webhodlela la..., le..., lo...***
	oohaa:foo weboȴe:laa laa..., le..., lo...
a bottle of...	**ibhodlela la..., le..., lo...***
	eeboȴe:laa laa..., le..., lo...
a glass of...	**ingilazi ya..., ye..., yo...***
	eengeelaa:zee yaa..., ye..., yo...

Weights

100 grams of...	**amagremu angu-100 a..., e..., o...*** aamaagre:moo aangoo100 aa..., e..., o...
1/2 kilo of...	**uhhafu wekhilogremu la..., le..., lo...*** oohaa:foo wekeelogre:moo laa..., le..., lo...
a kilo of...	**ikhilogremu la..., le..., lo...*** eekeelogre:moo laa..., le..., lo...

Food

a slice of...	**ucezu lwa..., lwe..., lo...*** oo/ʔe:zoo lwaa..., lwe..., lo...
a portion of...	**ingxenye ya..., ye..., yo...*** eeŋ//gee:nye yaa..., ye..., yo...
a dozen...	**idazini la..., le..., lo...*** eedaazee:nee laa..., le..., lo...
a box of...	**ibhokisi la..., le..., lo...*** eebogee:see laa..., le..., lo...
a packet of...	**iphakethe la..., le..., lo...*** eepage:te laa..., le..., lo...
a tin of...	**ithini la..., le..., lo...*** eetee:nee laa..., le..., lo...
a carton of...	**ikhathoni la..., le..., lo...*** eekaato:nee laa..., le..., lo...
a jar of...	**ujeke wa..., we..., wo...*** ooje:ge waa..., we..., wo...

Miscellaneous

50 rands worth of...	**amarandi angu-50 a..., e..., o...*** aamaaraa:ndee aangoo-50 aa..., e..., o...
a quarter	**ikota** eeko:taa
ten per cent	**amaphesenti ayishumi** aamaapese:ntee aayeeshoo:mee
more...	**ngaphezulu** ngaapezoo:loo
less...	**ngaphansi** ngaapaa:ntsee
enough of...	**-anele*** -aane:le
double	**ngokuphindiwe** ngogoopeendee:we
twice	**kabili** kaabee:lee

Numbers

As some numbers in Zulu can be rather long, it is acceptable to use the English numerals, in which case you pronounce the numbers in English. The Zulu versions of the numbers are nevertheless provided below as you may hear them when speaking to somebody in Zulu.

0	**iqanda**	ee!ˀaa:ndaa
1	**-nye**	-nye

2	**-bili** -bee:lee
3	**-thathu** -taa:too
4	**-ne** -ne
5	**-hlanu** -ɬaa:noo
6	**isithupha** eestoo:paa
7	**isikhombisa** eeskombee:saa
8	**isishiyagalombili** eessheeyaagaalombee:lee
9	**isishiyagalolunye** eessheeyaagaaloloo:nye
10	**ishumi** eeshoo:mee
11	**ishumi nanye** eeshoo:mee naa:nye
12	**ishumi nambili** eeshoo:mee naambee:lee
13	**ishumi nantathu** eeshoo:mee naantaa:too
14	**ishumi nane** eeshoo:mee naa:ne
15	**ishumi nanhlanu** eeshoo:mee naanɬaa:noo
16	**ishumi nesithupha** eeshoo:mee nestoo:paa
17	**ishumi nesikhombisa** eeshoo:mee neskombee:saa
18	**ishumi nesishiyagalombili** eeshoo:mee nessheeyaagaalombee:lee
19	**ishumi nesishiyagalolunye** eeshoo:mee nessheeyaagaaloloo:nye
20	**amashumi amabili** aamaashoo:mee aamaabee:lee
21	**amashumi amabili nanye** aamaashoo:mee aamaabee:lee naa:nye
22	**amashumi amabili nambili** aamaashoo:mee aamaabee:lee naambee:lee
23	**amashumi amabili nantathu** aamaashoo:mee aamaabee:lee naantaa:too
30	**amashumi amathathu** aamaashoo:mee aamaataa:too

40	**amashumi amane**
	aamaashoo:mee aamaa:ne
50	**amashumi amahlanu**
	aamaashoo:mee aamaałaa:noo
60	**amashumi ayisithupha**
	aamaashoo:mee aayeestoo:paa
70	**amashumi ayisikhombisa**
	aamaashoo:mee aayeeskombee:saa
71	**amashumi ayisikhombisa nanye**
	aamaashoo:mee aayeeskombee:saa naa:nye
72	**amashumi ayisikhombisa nambili**
	aamaashoo:mee aayeeskombee:saa
	naambee:lee
80	**amashumi ayisishiyagalombili**
	aamaashoo:mee
	aayeessheeyaagaalombee:lee
81	**amashumi ayisishiyagalombili nanye**
	aamaashoo:mee
	aayeessheeyaagaalombee:lee naa:nye
82	**amashumi ayisishiyagalombili nambili**
	aamaashoo:mee aayeessheeyaa-
	gaalombee:lee naambee:lee
90	**amashumi ayisishiyagalolunye**
	aamaashoo:mee
	aayeessheeyaagaaloloo:nye
91	**amashumi ayisishiyagalolunye nanye**
	aamaashoo:mee
	aayeessheeyaagaaloloo:nye naa:nye
100	**ikhulu** eekoo:loo
110	**ikhulu neshumi** eekoo:loo neshoo:mee

110

200	**amakhulu amabili**	
	aamaakoo:loo aamaabee:lee	
250	**amakhulu amabili namashumi amahlanu**	
	aamaakoo:loo aamaabee:lee naamaashoo:mee aamaaɬaa:noo	
1,000	**inkulungwane** eenkooloongwaa:ne	
1 million	**isigidi** eesgee:dee	

Days and months
• •

If you want to say a date in Zulu, you can use the phrase '**ngomhla ka-... ku...**'. 'On the 6th of November', for example, is '**ngomhla ka-6 kuNovemba**'.

Days

Monday	**uMsombuluko**	oomsombooloo:go
Tuesday	**uLwesibili**	oolwesbee:lee
Wednesday	**uLwesithathu**	oolwestaa:too
Thursday	**uLwesine**	oolwesee:ne
Friday	**uLwesihlanu**	oolwesɬaa:noo
Saturday	**uMgqibelo**	oom!ǵeebe:lo
Sunday	**iSonto**	eeso:nto

If you want to say 'on Monday/on Tuesday...' in Zulu, you prefix '**nga-**' to the Zulu forms.*

Seasons

spring	**intwasahlobo**	eentwaasaaɬo:bo
summer	**ihlobo**	eeɬo:bo
autumn	**ikwindla**	eegwee:nǀɣaa
winter	**ubusika**	ooboosee:gaa

If you want to say 'in spring/in summer...' in Zulu, you replace the initial vowel of the word for the season with an '**e-**'.

Months

January	**uJanuwari**	oojaanoowaa:ree
February	**uFebruwari**	oofebroowaa:ree
March	**uMashi**	oomaa:shee
April	**u-Ephreli**	ooepre:lee
May	**uMeyi**	oome:yee
June	**uJuni**	oojoo:nee
July	**uJulayi**	oojoolaa:yee
August	**u-Agasti**	ooaagaa:stee
September	**uSepthemba**	oosepte:mbaa
October	**u-Okthoba**	oo-okto:baa
November	**uNovemba**	oonove:mbaa
December	**uDisemba**	oodeese:mbaa

If you want to say 'in January/in February...', you prefix '**nga-**' to the Zulu word for the month.*

| What is today's date? | **Zingaki namuhla?** |
| | zeengaa:gee naamoo:ɬaa? |

It's the fifth of March	**Zingu-5 kuMashi** zeengoo5 koomaa:shee
It's 8th July 2008	**Zingu-8 kuJulayi 2008** zeengoo8 koojoolaa:yee 2008
1st January	**ngomhla ka-1 kuJanuwari** ngo:mɬaa kaa1 koojaanoowaa:ree
on Saturday	**ngoMgqibelo** ngom!ǵeebe:lo
on Saturdays	**ngeMigqibelo** ngemee!ǵeebe:lo
every Saturday	**ngayo yonke iMigqibelo** ngaa:yo yo:nke eemee!ǵeebe:lo
this Saturday	**ngalo Mgqibelo** ngaa:lo m!ǵeebe:lo
next Saturday	**ngoMgqibelo ozayo** ngom!ǵeebe:lo ozaa:yo
last Saturday	**ngoMgqibelo odlule** ngom!ǵeebe:lo oɮoo:le
in June	**ngoJuni** ngojoo:nee
at the beginning of June	**ekuqaleni kukaJuni** egoo:lʔaale:nee koogaajoo:nee
at the end of June	**ekupheleni kukaJuni** egoopele:nee koogaajoo:nee
before the summer	**ngaphambi kwehlobo** ngaapaa:mbee kweɬo:bo
during the summer	**ehlobo** eɬo:bo
after the summer	**emva kwehlobo** emvaa kweɬo:bo

Time

What time is it?	**Yisikhathi sini?**
	yeeskaatee see:nee?
It's one o'clock	**Yihora lokuqala**
	yeeho:raa logoo!ˀaa:laa
It's two o'clock	**Yihora lesibili**
	yeeho:raa lesbee:lee
It's six o'clock	**Yihora lesithupha**
	yeeho:raa lestoo:paa
morning	**ekuseni**
	egoose:nee
It's midday	**Kusemini**
	koosemee:nee
afternoon	**ntambama**
	ntaambaa:maa
evening	**kusihlwa**
	koosee:ɬwaa
night	**ebusuku**
	eboosoo:goo
It's midnight	**Kuphakathi kwamabili**
	koopaagaa:tee kwaamaabee:lee
9	**Ngu-9**
	ngoo9
9.10	**Ngu-9.10**
	ngoo9.10
quarter past 9	**Ngu-9.15**
	ngoo9.15
9.20	**Ngu-9.20**
	ngoo9.20

9.30	**Ngu-9.30**
	ngoo9.30
9.35	**Ngu-9.35**
	ngoo9.35
quarter to 10	**Ngu-9.45**
	ngoo9.45
10 to 10	**Ngu-9.50**
	ngoo9.50

Time phrases

When does it open/close/ begin/finish?	**Kuvulwa, Kuvalwa, Kuqalwa, Kuqedwa ngasikhathi sini?**
	koovoo:lwaa, koovaa:lwaa, koo!ʔaa:lwaa, koo!ʔe:dwaa ngaaskaa:tee see:nee?
at three o'clock	**ngo-3**
	ngo3
before three o'clock	**ngaphambi kuka-3**
	ngapaa:mbee koogaa3
after three o'clock	**emva kuka-3**
	e:mvaa koogaa3
today	**namhlanje**
	naamɬaa:nje
tonight	**namhlanje ebusuku**
	naamɬaa:nje eboosoo:goo
tomorrow	**kusasa**
	koosaa:saa
yesterday	**izolo**
	eezo:lo

Eating out

In a coffee shop
• •

Coffee shops serve a wide variety of drinks but
specialise in coffees. Cakes and light meals are
normally also available.

Caffé Latte	**i-Caffé Latte**
	eecaffé latte
Espresso	**i-Espresso**
	ee-espresso
filter coffee	**i-Filter coffee**
	eefilter coffee
decaffeinated coffee	**ikhofi elingena-caffeine**
	eeko:fee eleengenacaffeine
coffee with hot milk	**ikhofi elinobisi olushisayo**
	eeko:fee eleenobee:see oloosheesaa:yo
Cappuccino	**ikhaphushino**
	eekaapooshee:no
a coffee	**ikhofi**
	eeko:fee
a smoothie	**i-smoothie**
	eesmoothie

A Ungathandani?
oongaataandaa:nee?
What will you have?

B Ngicela itiye elinobisi.
ngee/ˀe:laa eetee:ye eleenobee:see.
A tea with milk, please.

an orange juice	**ujusi wamawolintshi**
	oojoo:see waamaawolee:nchee
with lemon	**nolamula**
	nolaamoo:laa
no sugar	**ungawufaki ushukela**
	oongaawoofaa:gee ooshooge:laa
for two	**kwabantu ababili**
	kwaabaa:ntoo aabaabee:lee
for me	**kwami ngedwa**
	kwaa:mee nge:dwaa
for him/her	**kwakhe**
	kwaa:ke
for us	**kwethu**
	kwe:too
with ice, please	**ngicela ufane no-ayisi**
	ngee/ˀe:laa oofaa:ne
	noaayee:see
Some mineral water	**Amanzi esiphethu**
	aamaa:ndzee espe:too
Some sparkling mineral water	**Amanzi esiphethu azoyizayo**
	aamaa:ndzee espe:too
	aazoyeezaa:yo

Some still mineral water	**Amanzi esiphethu avamile**
	aamaa:ndzee espe:too
	aavaamee:le

Other drinks to try

hot chocolate	**ushokoledi oshisayo**
	ooshokole:dee osheesaa:yo
milkshake	**i-milkshake**
	eemilkshake
Rooibos tea	**itiye le-Rooibos**
	eetee:ye lerooibos

In a restaurant

I'd like to book a table for ... people	**Ngingathanda ukubhuka itafula labantu abangu-...**
	ngeengaataa:ndaa
	oogooboo:gaa eetaafoo:laa
	laabaa:ntoo aabaango...
for tonight	**namhlanje ebusuku**
	naam+aa:nje eboosoo:goo
for tomorrow night	**kusasa ebusuku**
	koosaa:saa eboosoo:goo
for 7.30	**ngo-7.30**
	ngo7.30
The menu, please	**Ngicela imenu**
	ngee/ʔe:laa eemenu
What is the dish of the day?	**Isidlo sanamhlanje siyini?**
	eesee:ɮo saanaam+aa:nje
	seeyee:nee?

I'll have the set menu at ... Rand, please	**Ngizothatha imenu elibiza amarandi angu-...**
	ngeezotaa:taa eemenu eleebee:zaa aamaaraa:ndee aangoo...
Can you recommend a local dish?	**Yisiphi isidlo esithandwayo endaweni osaziyo?**
	yeesee:pee eesee:ɓo eseetaandwaa:yo endaawe:nee osaazee:yo?
What is in this?	**Kwenziwe ngani lokhu kudla?**
	kwendzee:we ngaa:nee lo:koo goo:ɓaa?
I'll have this	**Ngicela lokhu**
	ngee/ʔe:laa lo:koo
More bread...	**Ngicela esinye isinkwa...**
	ngee/ʔe:laa esee:nye eesee:nkwaa...
More water...	**Ngicela amanye amanzi...**
	ngee/ʔe:laa aamaa:nye aamaa:ndzee
please	**ngicela...**
	ngee/ʔe:laa...
The bill, please	**Ngizokhokha malini?**
	ngeezoko:kaa maalee:nee?
Is service included?	**Ingabe nesevisi ihlanganisiwe?**
	eengaa:be nesevee:see eeɬaangaaneesee:we?

Itafula labantu ababili? eetaafoo:laa laabaa:ntoo aabaabee:lee?	A table for two?

Vegetarian

•••••••••••••••••••••••••••••••••••••

South Africans love meat, but you should still be able
to find some vegetarian dishes on the menus of most
restaurants. If this is not the case, restaurants will
have salads on offer.

Are there any vegetarian restaurants here?	**Zikhona izitolo zokudlela zamazilanyama lapha?** zeeko:naa eezeeto:lo zogooʒe:laa zaamaazeelaanyaa:maa laa:paa?
Do you have any vegetarian dishes?	**Ninazo izidlo zezilanyama?** neenaa:zo eezee:ʒo zezeelaanyaa:maa?
Which dishes have no meat?	**Yiziphi izidlo ezingenanyama?** yeezee:pee eezee:ʒo ezeengenaanyaa:maa?
Which dishes have no fish?	**Yiziphi izidlo ezingenanhlanzi?** yeezee:pee eezee:ʒo ezeengenaan4aa:ndzee?

What fish dishes do you have?	**Ninaziphi izidlo zenhlanzi?**
	neenaazee:pee eezee:ʒo zen4aa:ndzee?
I'd like pasta as a main course	**Ngingathanda iphasta njengesidlo esikhulu**
	ngeengaataa:ndaa eepaa:staa njengesee:ʒo eseekoo:loo
I don't like meat	**Angiyithandi inyama**
	aangeeyeetaa:ndee eenyaa:maa
What do you recommend?	**Yisiphi isidlo esimnandi kakhulu osaziyo?**
	yeesee:pee eesee:ʒo eseemnaa:ndee kaakoo:loo osaazee:yo?
Is it made with vegetable stock?	**Ingabe kwenziwe ngenhlanganisela yemifino?**
	eengaa:be kwendzee:we ngen4aangaaneese:laa yemeefee:no?

Traditional dishes

South Africa has many different kinds of restaurants serving all kinds of dishes. Listed below are some traditional Zulu foods that will, however, not be found in most restaurants.

imifino cooked green herbs

isitambu stamped mealies mixed and cooked together with fresh beans. Sometimes some meat

or intestines are added to make this food more
palatable. Any spice can be added

ujeqe a very tasty bread made from crushed boiled
mealies

idombolo dumpling

isijabani green herbs are mixed with crushed mealies
so as to form a soft mash

isijingi usually a thick porridge made of meal and
pumpkin boiled together

amadumbe edible tuber of the arum lily family. Most
palatable when eaten with salt

uphuthu thick, loose porridge. This is most popular
and can be eaten with meat and soup or replaces
rice. Some people prefer eating '**uphuthu**' with
'**amasi**' (sour milk)

usu intestines – very popular food

Wines

South Africa has a wide variety of wines. The list in
this section is just a general overview of some of the
wines available.

white wine	**iwayini elimhlophe**
	eewaayee:nee eleem⊦o:pe
red wine	**iwayini elibomvu**
	eewaayee:nee eeleebo:mvoo
The wine list, please	**Ngicela uhlu lwamawayini**
	ngee/ʔe:laa oo:⊦oo lwaamaawaayee:nee

Can you recommend a good wine?	**Yiliphi iwayini elingcono olaziyo?**
	yeelee:pee eewaayee:nee eleeŋ/go:no olaazee:yoo?
A bottle of the house wine	**Ibhodlela lewayini lesitolo sokudlela**
	eeboʒe:laa lewaayee:nee lesto:lo sogooʒe:laa

Blanc de Blanc dry white wine
Cabernet Sauvignon dry red wine
Chardonnay fruity dry white wine
Chenin Blanc very dry white wine
Johannisberger full-bodied sweet white wine
Special Late Harvest sweet white wine
Merlot dry red wine
Pinotage dry red wine
Premier Grand Cru dry white wine
Rosé a range of these are available
Sauvignon Blanc fruity dry white wine
Shiraz dry red wine
Sparkling wine a variety of these are available
Stein semi-sweet white wine

Spirits and liqueurs

There are many different kinds of liqueurs and spirits on sale. Some examples are provided below.

What liqueurs do you have?	**Ninazo izinyembezi zikakhwini ezinjani?** neenaa:zo eezeenyembe:zee zeegaakwee:nee ezeenjaa:nee?

Amarula cream liqueur made from the fermented fruit of the Marula tree

Brandy

Cape Chocolate cream liqueur

Cape Marula cream liqueur

Cape Strawberry cream liqueur

Cape Velvet cream liqueur in different flavours such as English Toffee and Strawberry

Mampoer very strong clear alcoholic drink often made from fruit

Sherry

Van der Hum citrus-flavoured liqueur

Wild Africa Cream liqueur made from caramel and cream

Wild Nectar Honey golden-coloured honey liqueur

Wildebraam Youngberry rich liqueur made from youngberry juice

Witblits strong brandy distilled from grapes

Grammar

Zulu uses a conjunctive way of writing which means that an English sentence like 'I like you' is one word in Zulu – **'Ngiyakuthanda'**. Certain Zulu words therefore hardly ever appear on their own. In this phrasebook these words are preceded by a hyphen to indicate that they need a prefix.

Zulu also uses subject prefixes which link certain words to the noun in the sentence. This means that a noun and a verb hardly ever appear next to each other without this linking prefix. For example:
'The cat is eating' is **Ikati *li*yadla**
(**ikati** = noun, **-dla** = verb, **li-** = subject prefix)
'The dog is eating' is **Inja *i*yadla**
(**inja** = noun, **-dla** = verb, **i-** = subject prefix)

Nouns

Nouns are divided into classes which determine the type of prefix to be used when other words are linked to it e.g. **'um-'** is the class prefix in the word **'*um*fula'** ('river'). Many of the noun classes appear in singular and plural pairs. Plurals in Zulu are thus formed not by changing the endings of nouns but by changing the class prefix.

Vocative

When you speak to someone in Zulu, you omit the first letter of the name or noun you are using, eg. when you address somebody as 'Sir', you say **'Mnumzane'** instead of **'uMnumzane'**. This rule applies to all proper names as well. When you talk about somebody you say, **'UPeter ulambile'** ('Peter is hungry'), but when you ask, 'Peter, are you hungry?', you say, **'Peter, ulambile?'**.

Possessives

In Zulu, instead of saying 'my suitcase', you say 'suitcase of mine' (**'isutikesi lami'**). Possessives contain possessive prefixes that link the possession to the possessor. The possessive prefix has been highlighted in the following examples. (Notice that slight changes sometimes occur to the possessive prefix once it has combined with the possessor.)

izicathulo *za*kho (izicathulo *za-* + -kho)
your shoes = shoes **of** yours
ukudla *kwe*thu (ukudla *kwa-* + -ithu)
our food = food **of** ours
amaswidi *o*mntwana (amaswidi *a-* + umntwana)
the child's sweets = sweets **of** child

Some phrases containing possessives

above the door	ngaphezu *ko*mnyango
after breakfast	emva *kwe*bhulakufesi
before breakfast	ngaphambi *kwe*bhulakufesi
behind the door	emva *ko*mnyango

below the window	ngaphansi *kwe*fasitela
beside *(next to, by)* the river	eceleni *ko*mfula
between the men	phakathi *kwa*madoda
a bit (of) bread	ucezu *lwe*sinkwa
a bottle of water	ibhodlela *la*manzi
1/2 bottle of water	uhhafu *webhodlela la*manzi
a box of grapes	ibhokisi *la*magilebhisi
a carton of milk	ikhathoni *lo*bisi
a dozen eggs	idazini *la*maqanda
a glass of water/ wine/milk	ingilazi *ya*manzi, *ye*wayini, *yo*bisi
100 grams of meat	amagremu angu-100 enyama
in front of the shop	ngaphambi *kwe*sitolo
instead of coffee	esikhundleni *se*khofi
a jar of sugar	ujeke *ka*shukela
a kilo of meat	ikhilogremu *le*nyama
1/2 kilo of meat	uhhafu *wekhilogremu le*nyama
a litre of water	ilitha *la*manzi
more than the boys	ngaphezu *kwa*bafana
most (of) the girls	iningi *le*zintombi
next to the water	eceleni *kwa*manzi
a packet of pears	iphakethe *la*maganandoda
a portion of meat	ingxenye *ye*nyama
on top of the wall	phezu *ko*bonda
over *(on top of)* the bed	phezu *ko*mbhede
50 rands worth of meat	amarandi angu-50 enyama

a slice of bread	ucezu *lwe*sinkwa
a tin of mushrooms	ithini *la*makhowa
under the table	ngaphansi *kwe*tafula

The question 'Do you have...?' in Zulu consists of the following parts: '**U-**' (for one person), '**Ni-**' (for more than one person); '**-na-**' plus a suffix referring to the possession; and the possession. Compare the following examples:

Unabo abantwana?	Do you have children?
Yebo, *nginabo* abantwana.	Yes, I have children.
Ninalo ikamelo?	Do you have a room?
Yebo, *sinalo* ikamelo.	Yes, we have a room.

Locatives (denote place)

Zulu does not have prepositions such as 'at', 'on', 'in', 'into', 'to', 'from', 'out'. Instead, the locative is often used to convey these meanings. Locatives very often begin on '**e-**' and '**ku-**'. For example: '**esikhumulweni sezindiza**' ('at the airport'), '**kudokotela**' ('to the doctor') or '**kuSimon**' ('from Simon').

How to say 'with/by/made of'

'**Nga-**' is sometimes used to express 'with/by/made of'. See the following phrases:

| *by* (via) e-mail/phone | *nge*-email, *ngo*cingo |
| The chair is *made of* wood | Isihlalo senziwa *ngo*khuni |

'We **went/travelled by** car'   'Sihambe *nge*moto'
'**There's something**   'Kukhona inkinga
  wrong with the brakes'   *nga*mabhuleki'

Temporals (expressing the concept of time)
Time in Zulu can be expressed by means of '**nga-**'.
For example: 'on Tuesday' is '**ngoLwesibili**', while 'in
July' is '**ngoJulayi**'. Similarly, 'at 3 pm' is '**ngo-3 pm**'.

Verbs
• •

Verbs in Zulu only appear on their own when used as
a command. In all other cases they have a prefix.

Tenses
Present tense positive (nothing after verb)
(Noun) + subject prefix + **-ya-** + verb stem
Itekisi **liya**hamba.   The taxi is leaving.
Present tense positive (something after verb)
(Noun) + subject prefix + verb stem + object/adverb
Itekisi lihamba manje.   The taxi is leaving now.
Present tense negative
(Noun) + negative subject prefix + verb stem ending
on -**i** + (object/adverb)
Itekisi **ali**hambi manje.   The taxi is not leaving now.
Immediate past tense positive (nothing after verb)
(Noun) + subject prefix + verb stem ending on -**ile**
Ngi-odile.   I ordered.
Immediate past tense positive (something after verb)
(Noun) + subject prefix + verb stem ending on -**e** +
object/adverb

129

Ngi-*ode* iwayini.   I ordered wine.

Immediate past tense negative

(Noun) + negative subject prefix + verb stem ending
on -**anga** + (object/adverb)

Angi-*odanga*.   I didn't order.

Future tense positive

(Noun) + subject prefix + -**zo**-/-**yo**- + verb stem +
(object/adverb)

Sizo*ya* eThekwini.   We will go to Durban.

Future tense negative

(Noun) + negative subject prefix + -**zu**-/-**yu**- + verb
stem + (object/adverb)

Asi*zu*ya eThekwini.   We won't go to Durban.

Some phrases containing negatives:

I'm **allergic to** penicillin	**Angi**zwani nephenisilini
We **disagree**	**A**sivumelani
I saw **nobody**	**Angi**bon*anga* muntu
I saw him **nowhere**	**Angi**mbon*anga* ndawo
The telephone is **out of order**	Ucingo alusebenzi
I'm **single** (*unmarried*)	**Angi**shadile
He's **sober**	**Aka**dakiwe
It's **strange**	**Aku**jwayelekile
The man is **unemployed**	Indoda ayisebenzi
It is **unlikely**	**Aku**ngenzeki
It is **unpleasant**	**Aku**thokozisi
It is **vacant**	**Aku**namuntu
coffee **with no** (*without*) milk, sugar	ikhofi eli*ngena*bisi, eli*ngena*shukela

130

The telephone **doesn't work**	**Ucingo *alusebenzi***
The answer is **wrong**	**Impendulo *ayilungile***

Adjectives

• •

In Zulu, adjectives have to agree with the nouns that they are used with. For example:

ihhotela *elikhulu*	large hotel
isilwane *esincane*	small animal

'**-nye**' (also an adjective) is used for 'some more' and 'another'. Compare the following examples:

***olunye* ubisi**	some more milk
***elinye* ikamelo**	another room

Questions

• •

Sometimes a mere change of intonation will indicate that a question is being asked. In other cases, a prefix, suffix or question word must be used.

-phi? (where?)
Uhlala*phi*?	Where do you live?

-ni? (what?)
Uthengisa*ni*?	What are you selling?

-kuphi? (where is/are?)

Iposi li*kuphi*? Where is the post office?

-kuphi... -eduze? (where is the nearest...?)

Si*kuphi* isibhedlela es*iseduze*? Where is the nearest hospital?

-njani? (what kind?)

Nibone izilwane ezi*njani*? What kind of animals did you (plural) see?

-ngaki? (how many?)

Nifuna ama-apula ama*ngaki*? How many apples do you (plural) want?

-phi? (which (one)?/which (ones)?)

Uthanda mu*phi* umuthi? Which tree do you like?

Uthanda mu*phi*? Which one (i.e. tree) do you like?

nini? (when?)

Sizofika *nini* eThekwini? When will we arrive in Durban?

Other

Articles
Zulu doesn't have separate words for 'a(n)' and 'the'. Normally the context will determine whether the

noun is definite or indefinite. If you want to say 'a car', you will simply use the word for car, which is **'imoto'**.

Some

When 'some' is used as in 'I'd like some tea', it is not translated with a separate word. You can simply say **'Ngingathanda itiye'**.

Still

'-sa-' with verbs and **'-se-'** with non-verbs. For example: 'I'm still eating' is **'Ngisadla'**, while 'The grass is still green' is **'Utshani buseluhlaza'**.

More phrases with an asterisk.

and water	namanzi
Swimming is ***better*** ***(than)*** sailing	Ukubhukuda kungcono kunokuntweza
The elephant is ***bigger*** ***(than)*** the black rhino	Indlovu inkulu kunobhejane
concerning/about/ *re* the company	mayelana nenkampani
I will ***consult*** a doctor	Ngizobonana nodokotela
How much are the watermelons/ bananas *each*?	Limalini ikhabe ngalinye?, Umalini ubhanana ngamunye?
enough food	ukudla okwanele
Here are the buses	Nanka amabhasi
Here is the hospital	Nasi isibhedlela
Chips cost *less than* sweets	Amashibusi abiza kancanyana kunamaswidi

I've lost the car key/our luggage	Ngilahlekelwe yisikhiye semoto, ngumthwalo wethu
I *missed* the plane	Ngishiywe yibhanoyi
near the water/bus/river	eduze namanzi, nebhasi, nomfula
one lion/elephant	ibhubesi elilodwa, indlovu eyodwa
opposite the children/hospital/tree	malungana nabantwana, nesibhedlela, nomuthi
per day	ngosuku
This is *similar (to)* soup	Lokhu kufana nesobho
I will *talk (to)* the police	Ngizokhuluma namaphoyisa
that car/*that (one)* i.e. car	leyo moto, leyo
There are the buses	Nanko amabhasi
There is the hospital	Naso isibhedlela
these cars/*these (ones)* i.e. cars	lezi zimoto, lezi
this car/*this (one)* i.e. car	le moto, le
those cars/*those (ones)* i.e. cars	lezo zimoto, lezo
with the men/girls/boy	namadoda, nezintombi, nomfana

134

Culture and customs

'Ilobolo' was a way in which the bridegroom showed gratitude towards his bride's parents. Cattle, among other things, were originally used to pay **'ilobolo'**, while money is used nowadays. Some Zulus today, however, prefer not to get married and just have partners.

Respect has always been an integral part of Zulu culture. **'Ubuntu'** is a term that reminds a person of the obligation to show respect to others. Among other things, **'ubuntu'** is expressed by greeting everybody and by showing hospitality even to strangers.

cattle enclosure	**isibaya**
	eesbaa:yaa
dance	**umgido**
	oomgee:do
herbalist	**usomakhambi**
	oosomaakaa:mbee
king/chief	**inkosi**
	eenko:see
grindstone	**itshe lokugaya**
	ee:che logoogaa:yaa
stick-fight	**ukungcweka**
	oogooŋ/gwe:gaa
traditional village	**isigodi**
	eesgo:dee

I would like to taste...	**Ngingathanda ukunambitha...**
	ngeengaataa:ndaa
	oogoonaambee:taa...
some curdled milk	**amasi**
	aamaa:see
some traditional beer	**utshwala**
	oochwaa:laa

Old names and new names

The names of some towns and cities in South Africa have officially been changed, while others are still in the process of being changed. On older maps and even on some signboards you may still find the old names of places.

Old name	*New name*
Ellisras	Lephalale
Louis Trichardt	Makhado
Messina	Musina
Naboomspruit	Moogkophong
Nylstroom	Modimolle
Pietersburg	Polokwane
Potgietersrus	Mokopane
Warmbaths	Bela-Bela

Some people are advocating the name **'Tshwane'** for Pretoria. Many street names have also been changed. You may sometimes still find the old names in older maps and on some signboards.

Zulu place names

Many places in South Africa have Zulu equivalents that are used when speaking Zulu. In some cases, the Zulu names are very similar to those that you would use in English, but in other cases the Zulu versions are totally different. You will almost always use place names in the form in which they occur below, i.e. starting with 'e-'.

Durban	**eThekwini**
Dundee	**eDandi**
East London	**eMonti**
Ermelo	**eMlomo**
Estcourt	**eMtshezi**
Johannesburg	**eGoli, eJozi**
Cape Town	**eKapa**
Kimberley	**eKhimbali**
Ladysmith	**eMnambithi**
Middelburg	**eMhluzi**
Nelspruit	**eNasipothi**
Newcastle	**eNyukhasela**
Pietermaritzburg	**eMgungundlovu**
Port Elizabeth	**eBhayi**
Port Shepstone	**eSayidi**
Pretoria	**ePitoli**
Witbank	**eMalahleni**

A

English	Zulu	Pronunciation
a(n)	(see Grammar section)	
able: to be able to	...kwazi uku...	...gwaa:zee
about (approx.)	cishe	/ʔee:she
above	*	
abroad	phesheya	peshe:yaa
to accept	-amukela	-aamooge:laa
accident	ingozi	eengo:zee
accident & emergency unit (A&E)	umnyango wezingozi nezimo eziphuthumayo	oomnyaa:ngo wezeengo:zee nezee:mo ezeepootoo-maa:yo
accommodation	indawo yokuhlala	eendaa:wo yogooɬaa:laa
to accompany	-phelekezela	-pelegeze:laa
account	i-akhawunti	eeakaawoo:ntee
to ache	-qaqamba	-ʔaʔʔaa:mbaa

English	Zulu	Pronunciation
it aches	kuyaqaqamba	kooyaa-ʔaaʔʔaa:mbaa
address	ikheli	eeke:lee
what is the address?	lithini ikheli?	leetee:nee eekee:lee?
admission	imali	eemaa:lee
charge	yokungena	yogoonge:naa
adult	umuntu	oomoo:ntoo
	okhulile	okoolee:le
to advise	-eluleka	-eloole:gaa
aeroplane	ibhanoyi	eebaano:yee
afraid: to be afraid of	-esaba	-esaa:baa
after	*	
afternoon: in the afternoon	ntambama	ntaambaa:maa
this afternoon	namhlanje	naamɬaa:nje
	ntambama	ntaambaa:maa
again	futhi	foo:tee
against	ngokumelene	ngoogoomele:ne
age	ubudala	ooboodaa:laa

English	Zulu	Pronunciation
ago: *a week ago*	ngesonto eledlule	ngeso:nto eletʃoo:le
ago		
to agree	-vumelana	-voomelaa:naa
air-conditioning	ukupholiswa nokufudunyezwa komoya	ukupholiswa:swaa nogoofoodoonyezwaa komoyaa
airplane	ibhanoyi	eebaano:yee
airport	isikhumulo sezindiza	eeskoomoo:lo sezeendee:zaa
airport bus	ibhasi lasesikhumulweni sezindiza	eebaa:see laaseskoomoolwe:nee sezeendee:zaa
air ticket	ithikithi lebhanoyi	eeteegee: tee lebaano:yee
alarm clock	iwashi elicushwayo	eewa:shee elee/ooshwaa:yo
alcohol	isidaki	eesdaa:gee
alcohol-free	-ngenasidaki	-ngenaasdaa:gee
all	-onke	-onke
allergic	*	*
allergy	i-aleji	eale:jee
to allow	vumela	-voome:laa
all right (agreed)	kulungile	kooloongee:le
are you all right?	uphila kahle?	oope:laa kaa:ɬe?
almost	-cishe	-ʔee:she
alone	-dwa	-dwaa
already	kakade	kaagaa:de
also	futhi	foo:tee
always	njalo	njaa:lo
a.m.	am	am
ambulance	i-ambhulense	eeamboole:ntse
America	imelika	eemelee:kaa
American	ummelikana	oommeleekaanaa
and	futhi*	foo:tee
angry	-thukuthele	-toogoote:le
another	-nye	-nye
answer	impendulo	eempendoo:lo
to answer	-phendula	-pendoo:laa

English - Zulu

English	Zulu	Pronunciation
answerphone	umshini wokuphendula ucingo	oomshee:nee wogoopendoo:-laa oo//ee:ngo
antacid	isihlambululisisu	eestaamboo-loo:lee see:soo
antibiotic	umuthi obulala amagciwane	oomoo:tee oboolaa:laa aamaa-/geewaa:ne
antihistamine	umuthi olwa ne-aleji	oomoo:tee o:lwaa neale:jee
antiseptic	isibulala magciwane	eesboolaa:laa maa/geewaa:ne
any	noma ikuphi	no:maa eegoo:pee
anyone	noma ngubani	no:maa ngoobaa:nee
anything	noma yini	no:maa yee:nee
apartment	ifulethi	eefle:tee
apple	i-apula	eeaapoo:laa
appointment	isikhathi sokubonana	eeskaa:tee sogoobonaa:naa

English	Zulu	Pronunciation
approximately	cishe	/ʔee:she
April	u-ephreli	oopre:lee
arm	ingalo	eengaa:lo
to arrange	-hlela	-te:laa
arrival	ukufika	oogoofee:gaa
to arrive	-fika	-fee:gaa
to ask (a question)	-buza	-boo:zaa
(request something)	-cela	-/ʔe:laa
aspirin	i-aspirini	eeaspeeree:nee
asthma	isifuba somoya	eesfoo:baa somo:yaa
I have asthma	ngiphethwe yisifuba somoya	ngeepe:twe yeesfoo:baa somo:yaa
at	*	
at 8 o'clock	ngo-8	ngo8
at my/your home	ekhaya lami, lakho	ekaa:yaa laa:mee, laa:ko
at night	ebusuku	eboosoo:goo

attack	ukuhlasela	oogoo4aase:laa
to attack	-hlasela	-4aase:laa
attractive	-khangayo	-kaangaa:yo
August	u-Agasti	ooaagaa:stee
Australia	i-Australia	eeaustraalia
Australian	umAustralia	oomaustraalia
automatic	ngokuzenza-	ngogoozendzaa-
	kalelayo	gaalelaa:yo
autumn	ikwindla	eegwee:n̄gaa
available	-tholakala	-tolaagaa:laa
to avoid	-gwema	-gwe:maa

B

baby	umntwana	umntwaa:naa
baby milk	ubisi	oobee:see
baby's bottle	ibhodlela	eebolge:laa
babysitter	umntwana	lomntwaa:naa
baby wipes	umzanyana	oomzaanyaa:naa
	okokusula	ogogoosoo:laa
	umntwana	oomntwaa:naa

back (of body)	umhlane	oom4aa:ne
backpack	ujosaka	oojosaa:gaa
bad	-bi	-bee
bag	isikhwama	eeskwaa:maa
baggage	umthwalo	oomtwaa:lo
bank	ibhange	eebaa:nge
bank account	ugu lomfula	oo:goo lomfoo:laa
	i-akhawunti	eeakaawoo:ntee
banknote	imali eyiphepha	yaasebhange yaasebaa:nge
		eemaa:lee
		eyeepe:paa
bar	inkantini	eenkaantee:nee
bath	ubhavu	oobaa:voo
bathroom	ibhavulumu	eebaavooloo:moo
battery	ibhethri	eebe:tree
B&B	i-B&B	eeb&b
to be	ukuba	oogoo:baa
beach	ibhishi	eebee:shee
bean	ubhontshisi	oobonchee:see
beautiful	isimomondiya	eesmomondeeyaa

English - Zulu

English	Zulu	Pronunciation
because	ngenxa yokuthi	nge:ŋ/aa yogoo:tee
to become	-ba	-baa
bed	umbhede	oombe:de
double bed	umbhede oyidabuli	oombe:de oyeedaaboo:lee
single bed	umbhede oyisingili	oombe:de oyeeseengee:lee
twin beds	imibhede ehlangene	eemeebe:de e4aange:ne
bedroom	ikamelo lokulala	eekaame:lo logoolaa:laa
	ubhiya	oobee:yaa
beer	*	
before	-qala	-ʔaalaa
beginner	imfunda-makhwelo	eemfoondaa-maakwe:lo
to begin	*	
behind	-kholwa	-ko:lwaa
to believe	*	
below	*	
beside (next to)	*	

English	Zulu	Pronunciation
best	-ngcono ukwedlula konke	-ŋ/go:no oogwegoo:laa ko:nke
better (than)	*	
between	*	
bicycle	ibhayisikili	eebaayee-seegee:lee
bicycle pump	iphampu yebhayisikili	eepaa:mpoo yebaayee-seegee:lee
big	-khulu	-koo:loo
bigger (than)	*	
bill	i-akhawunti	eeakaawoo:ntee
bin (dustbin)	umgqomo wezibi	oomlgo:mo wezee:bee
bird	inyoni	eenyo:nee
birthday	usuku lokuzalwa	ooso:goo logoozaa:lwaa
happy birthday	halala ngosuku lwakho lokuzalwa	haalaa:laa ngosoo:goo lwaa:ko logoozaa:lwaa

English	Zulu		English	Zulu
biscuits	amabhiskidi	aamaabee-skee:dee	blood pressure	umfutho wegazi	oomfoo:to wegaa:zee
bit: *a bit (of)*	*		blood test	ukuhlolwa kwegazi	oogoo+o:lwaa kwegaa:zee
bite (animal)	ukulunywa yisilwane	oogooloo:nywaa yeeseelwaa:ne	blouse	ibhulawuzi	eeblaawoo:zee
(insect)	ukulunywa yisinambuzane	oogooloo:nywaa yeesnaamboo-zaa:ne	blow-dry	-omisa	-omee:saa
			blue	-luhlaza	-loo+aa:zaa
to bite (animal)	-luma	-loo:maa	to board (plane, train, etc.)	-gibela	-geebe:laa
bitten	-lunyiwe	-loonyee:we	boarding card	ikhadi	eekaa:dee
bitter	-baba	-baa:baa		lokugibela	logoogeebe:laa
black	-mnyama	-mnyaa:maa	boat	isikebhe	eeske:be
blanket	ingubo	eengoo:bo	(rowing)	isikebhe	eeske:be
to bleed	-opha	-o:paa		esigwedlayo	eseegwe+gaa:yo
blind (person)	impumputhe	eempoompoo:te	body	umzimba	oomzee:mbaa
blister	ibhamuza	eebaamoo:zaa	to boil	-bila	-bee:laa
blocked	-vinjiwe	-veenjee:we	(cause to boil)	-bilisa	-beelee:saa
blood	igazi	eegaa:zee	bone	ithambo	eetaa:mbo
blood group	inhlobo yegazi	yega:zee	(fish)	umgogodla	oomgogo:tgaa
				wenhlanzi	wen+aa:ndzee
			book	incwadi	een/'waa:dee

English – Zulu

English	Zulu	Pronunciation
to book	-bhuka	-boo:gaa
booking	ukubhuka	oogooboo:gaa
booking office	ihhovisi	eehovee:see
	lokubhuka	logooboo:gaa
bookshop	isitolo	eesto:lo
	sezincwadi	sezeerj:waa:dee
boots	amabhuthi	aamaaboo:tee
(short)	amabhuthi	aamaaboo:tee
	amafushane	aamaafooshaane
boring	-dina	-dee:naa
born: to be born	-zalwa	-zaa:lwaa
to borrow	-boleka	-bole:gaa
both	...bili	...bee:lee
bottle	ibhodlela	eebotje:laa
a bottle of water	ibhodlela	eebotje:laa
	lamanzi	laamaa:ndzee
bottle opener	isikulufu	eeskooloo:foo
	sokuvula	sogoovoo:laa
bottom (of pool, etc.)	ibhodlela	eebotje:laa
	iphansi	eepaa:ntsee

English	Zulu	Pronunciation
box office	ihhovisi	eehovee:see
	lokuthengisa	logootengee:saa
	amathikithi	aamaateegee:tee
boy	umfana	oomfaa:naa
boyfriend	isoka	eeso:gaa
to brake	-bhuleka	-boole:gaa
bread	isinkwa	eesee:nkwaa
bread roll	ibhanisi	eebaanee:see
to break	-phula	-poo:laa
breakdown	usizo	oosee:zo
van	lokudonswa	logoodo:ntswa
	kwemoto	kwemo:to
breakfast	ibhulakufesi	eeboolagoofe:see
breast	ibele	eebe:le
to breast-feed	-ncelisa	-nj/elee:saa
to breathe	-phefumula	-pefoomoo:laa
bride	umakoti	oomaako:tee
bridegroom	umkhwenyana	oomkwenyaa:naa
bridge	ibhuloho	eeblo:ho
briefcase	iputumende	eepootoome:nde
to bring	-letha	-le:taa

English	Zulu	Pronunciation
Britain	iNgilandi	eengeela:ndee
British	iNgisi	eengee:see
brochure	incwajana	een/waajaa:naa
broken	-phukile	-poogee:lee
broken down (car, etc.)	-phukile	-poogee:le
bronchitis	umkhuhlane wamaphaphu	oomkoo4aa:ne waamaapaa:poo
brother	umfowethu	oomfowe:too
brother-in-law	usbari	oosbaa:ree
brown	-nsundu	-ntsoo:ndoo
bruise	ishandu	eeshaa:ndoo
buffet car (train)	inqola yesitimela ethengisa ukudla	eenlo:laa yesteeme:laa etengee:saa oogoo:ɓaa
to build	-akha	-aa:kaa
building	isakhiwo	eesaakee:wo
bulb (light)	ibhalbhu	eebaa:lboo
bunch (of flowers)	isikhawu sezimbali	ees//haa:woo sezeembaa:lee

English	Zulu	Pronunciation
(of grapes)	ihlukuzo lamagilebhisi	ee4oogoo:zo laamaageele-bee:see
bureau de change	isikhungo sokushintsha imali yakwamanye amazwe	eeskoo:ngo sogooshee:nchaa eemaa:lee yaagwaamaa:nye aamaa:zwe
burger	ibhega	eebe:gaa
burglar	umgqekezi	oomlgege:zee
to burn	-shisa	-shee:saa
bus	ibhasi	eebaa:see
bus station	isiteshi samabhasi	eeste:shee saamaabaa:see
bus stop	isitobhu samabhasi	eesto:boo saamaabaa:see
bus ticket	ithikithi lebhasi	eeteegee:tee lebaa:see
business	ibhizinisi	eebeezeenee:see
on business	-enza ibhizinisi	-e:ndzaa eebeezeenee:see

English – Zulu

English – Zulu

English	Zulu	Pronunciation
businessman/woman	usomabhizinisi	oosomaabee-zeenee:see
business trip	uhambo lwebhizinisi	oohaa:mbo lwe-beezeenee:see
busy	-matasa	-maataa:saa
but	kodwa	ko:dwaa
butter	ibhotela	eebote:laa
to buy	-thenga	-te:ngaa
by	*	
by bus	ngebhasi	ngebaa:see
by car	ngemoto	ngemo:to
by ship	ngomkhumbi	ngomkoo:mbee
by train	ngesitimela	ngesteeme:laa
C		
cab (taxi)	itekisi	eetegee:see
cabin (on boat)	ikamelo lokulala emkhunjini	eekaame:lo logoola:laa emkoonjee:nee
café	ikhefi	eeke:fee

internet café

English	Zulu	Pronunciation
internet café	izikhungo ze-inthanethi	eezeekoo:ngo ze-eentane:tee
cake (large)	ikhekhe elikhulu	eeke:ke eleekoo:loo
(small)	ikhekhe elincane	eeke:ke eleen/aa:ne
call (telephone)	ucingo	oo/?ee:ngo
to call (speak)	-biza	-bee:zaa
(phone)	shaya ucingo	shaayaa oo/?ee:ngo
calm	-thulile	-toolee:le
camera	ikhamera	eekame:raa
to camp	-khempa	-ke:mpaa
camping gas	igesi yokukhempa	eege:see yogooke:mpaa
campsite	indawo yokukhempa	eendaa:wo yogooke:mpaa
can		
(to be able to)	-yakwazi uku...	-yaagwaa:zee oogoo...
(to know how to)	-nga...	-ngaa...
I can	nginga...	ngeengaa...

English	Zulu	
we can	singa...	seengaa...
can	ithini	eetee:nee
Canada	iKhanada	eekana:daa
Canadian	umKhanada	oomkana:daa
to cancel	-khansela	-kantse:laa
cancellation	ukukhansela	oogookantse:laa
capital (city)	inhlokodolobha	een+ogodolo:baa
car	imoto	eemo:to
car alarm	i-alamu yemoto	eealaa:moo yemo:to
car hire	ukuqasha imoto	oogoo?aa:shaa eemo:to
car insurance	umshuwalense wemoto	oomshoowaale:-ntse wemo:to
car keys	isikhiye semoto	eeskee:ye semo:to
car park	indawo yokupaka izimoto	eendaa:wo yogoopaa:gaa eezeemo:to
car parts	izipele zemoto	eezeepe:le zemo:to
car seat (for child)	isihlalo semoto somntwana	ees4aa:lo semo:to somntwaa:naa
card	ikhadi	eekaa:dee
business card	ikhadi lebhizinisi	eekaa:dee lebeezeenee:see
careful: to be careful	-qaphela	-l?aape:laa
carriage (railway)	inqola	eenjo:laa
to carry	-thwala	-twa:laa
case (suitcase)	isutikesi	eesooteeke:see
to cash (cheque)	ukheshi	ooke:shee
cash desk/till	-khesha isheke	-ke:shaa eeshe:ge
cash dispenser (ATM)	ikhisi lemali	eekee:see lemaa:lee
	i-ATM	eeatm
casualty department	umnyango wabalimele	oomnyaa:ngo waabaaleeme:le
cat	ikati	eekaa:tee
to catch	-bamba	-baa:mbaa
cathedral	ikhathedrali	eekatheedraa:lee

English	Zulu	
Catholic	umKatolika	oomkaatolee:kaa
cave	umgede	oomge:de
cellphone	umakhalekhwini	oomaakaalekoo-kwee:nee
cent (euro)	isenti	eese:ntee
centimetre	isentimitha	eesenteemee:taa
central	maphakathi	maapaagaa:tee
central heating	isimiso sokufudumeza	eesmeeso sogoo-foodoome:zaa
central locking	isihluthulela zonke	eestootoole:laa zo:nke
centre	isikhungo	eeskoo:ngo
cereal	amasiriyeli	aamaaseereeyelee
certificate	istifiketi	eesteefeeke:tee
chair	isihlalo	eestaa:lo
champagne	ishampeni	eshaampe:nee
change (small coins)	ushintshi	ooshee:nchee
to change	-shintsha	-shee:nchaa
to change money	-shintsha imali	-shee:nchaa eemaa:lee

English	Zulu	
to change trains	-gibela isitimela esinye	geebe:laa eesteeme:laa esee:nye
charge (fee)	inkokhelo	eenkoke:lo
charge: I've run out of charge	ngiphelelwe ibhethri	ngeepele:lwe eebe:tree
to charge	-tshaja	-chaa.jaa
to charge a phone	-tshaja ucingo	-chaa.jaa oo/ee:ngo
cheap	-shibhile	-sheebee:le
to check	-hlola	-ło:laa
to check in (at hotel)	-ngena	-nge:naa
check-in (desk)	ukubhalisa	oogoobaalee:saa
cheers! (before drinking)	mpilonhle!	mpeelo:nłe!
(to one person staying behind)	sala kahle!	saa:laa kaa:łel
(to one person leaving)	hamba kahle!	haa:mbaa kaa:łel
chef	umpheki	oompe:gee

English	Zulu	Pronunciation
chemist's	ikhemisi	eekemee:see
cheque	isheke	eeshe:ge
cheque book	incwadi yamasheke	eenj/waa.dee yaamaashe:ge
cheque card	ikhadi lesheke	eekaa:dee leshe:ge
chest (body)	isifuba	eesfoo:baa
chicken	inkukhu	eenkoo:koo
child	umntwana	oomntwaa:naa
children	abantwana	aabaantwaa:naa
chilli (fruit)	upelepele	oopelepe:le
(dish)	isitshulu	eeschoo:loo
chips	seminsi	semee:ntsee
	esibabayo amashibusi	esbaabaa:yo aamaashee-boo:see
chocolate	ushokoledi	ooshogole:dee
drinking-chocolate	ushokoledi ophuzwayo	ooshogole:dee opoozwaa:yo
hot chocolate	ushokoledi oshisayo	ooshogole:dee osheesaa:yo
chocolates	oshokoledi	oshogole:dee
to choose	-khetha	-ke:taa
Christmas	uKhisimusi	ookeeseemoo:see
merry Christmas!	uKhisimusi omuhle!	ookeeseemoo:see omoo:4el
church	isonto	eeso:nto
cigarette	usikiidi	oosegeelee:dee
cigarette lighter	ilayitha	eelaayee:taa
cinema	ibhayisikobho	eebaayeesko:bo
city	idolobha	eedolo:baa
city centre	inkaba yedolobha	eenkaa:baa yedolo:baa
class	iklasi	eekeelaa:see
first class	ufesikilasi	oofeeseekeelaasee
second class	usekenikilasi	oosegeneekee-laa:see
clean	-hlanzekile	-4aandzegee:lee
to clean	-hlanza	-4aa-ndzaa
clear	-cwathile	-/'waatee:le
client	ikhasimende	eekaaseeme:nde

English – Zulu

English – Zulu

English	Zulu	Pronunciation
to climb	-qombola	-ʔombo:laa
clock	ikilogo	eekeelo:go
close by	eduze	edoo:ze
to close	-vala	-vaa:laa
closed (shop, etc.)	-valiwe	-vaalee:we
clothes	izingubo	eezeengoo:bo
clothes shop	isitolo	eesto:lo
cloudy	sezingubo	sezeengoo:bo
coach	-guqubele	-gooʔ/oobe:le
coast	ibhasi	eebaa:see
coat	ugu	oo:goo
cocoa	ijazi	eeja:zee
coffee	ukhokho	ooko:ko
black coffee	ikhofi	eeko:fee
white coffee	ikhofi	eeko:fee
	elimnyama	eleemnyaa:ma
	ikhofi elinobisi	eeko:fee eeleenobee:see
cappuccino	ikhaphushino	eekaapooshee:no
decaffeinated coffee	ikhofi elingena-caffeine	eeko:fee eleengena-naacaffeine

English	Zulu	Pronunciation
coin	uhlamvu	ooɬaa:mvoo
cold	iwemali	lwemaa:lee
I'm cold	-banda	-baa:ndaa
cold (illness)	ngiyagodola	ngeeyaagodo:laa
I have a cold	umkhuhlane	oomkooɬaa:ne
	nginomkhuhlane	ngeenomkoo-ɬaa:ne
cold sore	isilonda	eeslo:ndaa
	somkhuhlane	somkoɬaa:ne
colleague	umlingani	oomleenga:nee
to collect (someone)	-landa	-laa:ndaa
colour	umbala	oombaa:laa
to come (to arrive)	-fika	-fee:gaa
to come back	-buya	-boo:yaa
to come in	-ngena	-nge:naa
comfortable	-nethezekile	-netezege:le
company (firm)	ifemu	eefe:moo
compartment	ikhompathi-menti	eekompaatee-me:ntee

English	Zulu	
to complain	-khononda	-kono:ndaa
complaint	isikhalo	eeskaa:lo
to complete	-phothula	-potoo:laa
compulsory	-yimpoqo	-yeempo:!'o
computer	ikhompuyutha	eekompooyoota
concert	ikhonsathi	eekontsaa:tee
concession	isibonelelo	eesbonele:lo
condom	ikhondomu	eekondo:moo
conference	inkomfa	eenko:mfaa
to confirm	-qinisa	-!'eenee:saa
confirmation	isiqinisekiso	ees!'eeneese-gee:so
congratulations	umhalaliselo	oomhaalaaleeselo
congratulations!	halala!	haalaa:laa!
connection	isithuthi	eestoo:tee
(train, bus, etc.)		
consulate	sokuxhuma	sogoo//hoo:maa
	ihhovisi	eehovee:see
	likakhonsela	leegaakontse:laa
to consult	*	
to contact	-thintana	-teentaa:naa

English	Zulu	
contact lenses	ama-contact lense	aamaacontact lense
to continue	-qhubeka	-lhoobe:gaa
contraceptive	isivalanzalo	eesvaalaandzaa:lo
contract	isivumelwano	eesvoomelwaa:no
to cook	-pheka	-pe:gaa
(be cooking)		
cool	-pholile	-polee:le
copy (duplicate)	ikhophi	eeko:pee
to copy	-kopisha	-kopee:shaa
corkscrew	okokuvula ukhokhi	ogogoovoo:laa ooko:kee
corner	ikhona	eeko:naa
cornflakes	ama-cornflake	aamaacornflake
corridor	iphaseji	eepase:jee
cosmetics	izimonyo	eezeemo:nyo
cost	izindleko	eezeentje:go
to cost	-biza	-bee:zaa
how much does it cost?	kubiza malini?	koobee:zaa maalee:nee?

English – Zulu

English – Zulu

English	Zulu	Pronunciation
costume (swimming)	izingubo zokubhukuda	eezeengoo:bo zogooboo-goodaa
cough	umkhuhlane	oomkoo4aa:ne
cough mixture	umuthi womkhuhlane	oomoo:tee womkoo4aa:ne
to cough	-khwehlela	-kwete:laa
counter (shop, bar, etc.)	ikhawunta	eekaawoo:ntaa
country (nation)	izwe isizwe	ee:zwe eesee:zwe
countryside	amaphandle	aamaapaa:nŧe
couple (two people)	umbhangqwana	oombaa-nʒgwaa:naa
a couple of...	-mbalwa	-mbaa:lwaa
course (syllabus)	uhlelo lwezifundo	ooŧe:lo lwezeefoo:ndo
(of meal)	isigaba sokudla	eesgaa:baa soogoo:ʒgaa
cousin	umzala	oomzaa:laa
cover charge (restaurant)	i-cover charge	eecover charge
crafts	imisebenzi yezandla	eemeesebe:ndzee yezaa:nŧgaa
crash (car)	ukushayisa	oogooshaayeesaa
crash helmet	umakalabha	oomaagaalaa:baa
cream (food)	ukhilimu	ookeelee:moo
(lotion)	iloshini	eeloshee:nee
credit (on mobile phone)	isikweletu	eeskwele:too
crime	ubugebengu	ooboogebe:ngoo
crisps	amashibusi	aamaasheeboo:-see
cross (road, sea, etc.)	isiphambano	eespaambaa:no
to cross	-wela	-we:laa
crossing (by sea)	ukuwela	oogoowe:laa
crossroads	impambano yemigwaqo	eempaambaa:no yemeegwaa:!?o
crowd	isixuku	ees:/?oo:goo
crowded	-minyene	-meenye:ne

English	Zulu	Pronunciation
to cry (weep)	-khala	-kaa:laa
cup	inkomishi	eenkomee:shee
current (air, water, etc.)	umsinga	oomse:ngaa
customer	ikhasimende	eekaaseeme:'nde
customs (duty)	intela	eente:laa
to cut	-sika	-see:gaa
to cycle	-gibela ibhayisikili	-geebelaa eebaa:yeeseegee:lee
cystitis	isistisi	eeseestee:see

D

English	Zulu	Pronunciation
daily (each day)	-emihla ngemihla	-emee:4aa ngemee:4aa
dairy produce	umkhiqizo wobisi	oomkeeʔee:zo wobee:see
damage	-limaza	-leemaa:zaa
dance	umdanso	oomdaa:ntso
to dance	-dansa	-daa:ntsaa
danger	ingozi	eengo:zee
dangerous	-nengozi	-nengo:zee
dark	-mnyama uma kumnyama	-mnyaa:maa oomaa koomnyaa:maa
after dark	usuku idethi	oosoo:goo eede:tee
date (calendar) (social)	usuku	oosoo:goo
date of birth	lokuzalwa	logoozaa:lwaa
daughter	indodakazi	eendodaagaa:zee
daughter-in-law	umalokazana	oomaalogaa-zaa:naa
day	usuku	oosoo:goo
every day	imihla ngemihla	eemee:4aa ngemee:4aa
per day	ngosuku	ngosoo:goo
dead (animals)	-file	-fee:le
dead (humans)	-shonile	-shonee:lee
deaf	-yisithulu	-yeestoo:loo
dear (expensive)	-biza kakhulu	-bee:zaa kaakoo:loo
(in letter)	-thandekayo	-taandegaa:yo
debit card	i-debit card	eedebit card

English – Zulu

English – Zulu

debts	izikweletu
decaffeinated	-ngena-caffeine
December	uDisemba
to declare	-dalula
nothing to declare	akukho okungadalulwa
deep	-shona
delay	ukubambe zeleka
delayed	-bambekile
delicious	-mnandi kakhulu
dentist	udokotela wamazinyo
dentures	amazinyo okufakelwa
deodorant	i-deodorant
to depart	-hamba
department store	isitolo esineminyango ehlukene

	eezekwele:too
	-ngenaacaffeine
	oodeese:mbaa
	-daaloo:laa
	aagoo:ko ogoo-ngaadaaloo:lwaa
	-sho:naa
	oogoobaambe-zele:gaa
	-baambegee:le
	-mnaa:ndee kakoo:loo
	oodogtee:laa waamaazee:nyo
	aamaazee:nyo ogoofaage:lwaa
	eededoorant
	-haa:mbaa
	eesto:lo eseene-meenyaa:ngo e-looge:ne

departure	ukuhamba
departure lounge	indawo yokuhlalisa abantu abahambayo
to describe	-chaza
description	incazelo
desk (furniture)	ideski
desk (information)	ikhawunta lokwaziswa
dessert	uphuthini
details	imininingwane
detergent	umuthi wokuhlanza
to develop (photos)	-geza izithombe
diabetic	umuntu onesifo sikashukela

	oogoohaa:mbaa
	eenda:wo yogoo4aalee:saa aabaa:ntoo aa-baahaambaa:yo
	-/haa:zaa
	een//aaze:lo
	eede:skee
	eekaawoo:ntaa logwaazee:swaa
	oopootee:nee
	eemeenee-neengwaa:nee
	oomoo:tee wogoo4aa:ndzaa
	-ge:zaa eezeeto:mbe
	oomoo:ntoo onesee:fo see-gaashooge:laa

English	Zulu	Pronunciation
I'm diabetic	ngiphethwe yisifo sikashukela	ngeepe:twe yeese:fo see-gaashooge:laa
to dial	-shaya ucingo	-shaa:yaa oo/?ee:ngo
(a number)	ikhodi	eeko:dee
dialling code	yokushaya ucingo	yogooshaa:yaa oo/?ee:ngo
to die	-fa	-faa
diesel	udizili	oodeezee:lee
diet	idayethi	eedaaye:tee
I'm on a diet	ngiyadayetha	ngeeyaadaaye:taa
different	-hlukile	-hooge:le
difficult	-nzima	-ndzee:maa
dining room	indlu yokudlela	ee:nʈoo yogooʈe:laa
dinner (evening meal)	ukudla kwakusihla	oogoo:ʈɠaa kwaagoosee:ɬwaa
to have dinner	-dla ukudla kwakusihlwa	-ɠaa oogoo:ʈɠaa kwaagoosee:ɬwaa
direct (train, etc.)	-qondile	-!?ondee:le

English	Zulu	Pronunciation
directions	indlela	eeŋʈe:laa
to ask for directions	-cela indlela	-/?e:laa eeŋʈe:laa
directory (telephone)	ibhuku locingo	eeboo:goo lo/?ee:ngo
dirty	-ngcolile	-n/golee:le
disabled (person)	umuntu okhubazekile	oomoo:nto okoobaazegee:le
to disagree	*	
disco	idisko	eede:sko
discount	isaphulelo	eesaapoole:lo
to discover	-thola	-to:laa
disease	isifo	eesee:fo
district	isigodi	eesgo:dee
to disturb	-phazamisa	-paazaamee:saa
to dive	-tshuza	-choo:zaa
diversion	ukuphambukiswa	oogoopaamboo-gee:swaa
divorced	-divosile	-deevosee:le
dizzy	-nesiyezi	-nesye:zee
to do	-enza	-e:ndzaa

English – Zulu

English – Zulu

English	Zulu	Pronunciation
doctor	udokotela	oodogote:laa
documents	imibhalo	eemeebaa:lo
dog	inja	ee:njaa
dollar	idola	eedo:laa
domestic flight	ibhanoyi elindiza phakathi nezwe	eebano:yee eleendee:zaa paagaa:tee ne:zwe
door	umnyango	oomnyaa:ngo
double	-dabuli	-daaboo:lee
double bed	umbhede oyidabuli	oombe:de oyeedaaboo:lee
double room	ikamelo eliyidabuli	ekaame:lo elee-yeedaaboo:lee
down: to go down	-ehla	-e:4aa
downstairs	phansi esitezi	paantsee estezee
dress	ilokwe	eelo:gwe
to dress	-goka	-Igo:gaa
dressing (for food)	isithokelo	eestoge:lo

English	Zulu	Pronunciation
(for wound)	ibhandeshi	eebande:shee
drink	isiphuzo	eespoo:zo
to drink	-phuza	-poo:zaa
drinking water	amanzi okuphuza	aamaa:ndzee ogoopoo:zaa
to drive	-shayela	-shaaye:lee
driver (of car)	umshayeli	oomshaaye:lee
driving licence	ilayisense yokushayela	eelaayeese:ntse yogooshaayelaa
to drown	-minza	-mee:ndzaa
drug (medicine)	umuthi	oomoo:tee
drug (narcotics)	izidakamizwa	eezeedaagaa-mee:zwaa
drunk	-dakiwe	-daagee:we
dry	-omile	-omee:le
to dry	-omisa	-omee:saa
dry-cleaner's	ilondolo	eelondo:lo
during	ngesikhathi	ngeskaa:tee
duty-free	-ngakhokhelwa ntela	-ngaakoke:lwaa nte:laa

English	Zulu	
DVD player	isidlali ma-DVD	eestɡaa:lee maadvd
E		
each	*	
ear	indlebe	eentɡe:be
earlier	-phambidlana kungakephuzi	-paambee!ɓaanaa koongaage-poo:zee
to earn	-hola	-ho:laa
earphones	izifakwandlebeni	eezeefaagwaa-ntɡebe:nee
east	impumalanga	eempoomaa-laa:ngaa
Easter	ama-Ista	aamaae:staa
happy Easter!	ama-Ista amahle!	aamaae:staa aama:!el
easy	-lula	-loo:laa
to eat	-dla	-ɓaa
egg	iqanda	ee!ʔaa:ndaa
either ... or	noma	no:maa
electric	-kagesi	-kaage:see

English	Zulu	
electricity	ugesi	ooge:see
electronic	ama-electronic	aamaaelectronic
elevator	ilifti	eelee:ftee
e-mail	i-e-mail	ee-email
to e-mail	-thumela i-e-mail	-toome:laa ee-email
e-mail address	ikheli ie-e-mail	eekee:lee le-email
embassy	inxusa	een//oo:saa
emergency	isimo esi-phuthumayo	eesee:mo esee-pootoomaa:yo
emergency exit	umnyango wokuphulu-kundlela	oomnyaa:ngo wogoopooloo-goontɡe:laa
empty	-nalutho	-naaloo:to
end	isigcino	ees//gee:no
engaged (to be married)	-thembisene	-tembee:ne
(phone, etc.)	umshado	oomshaa:do
(toilet)	-matasa	-maataa:saa
engine	-nomuntu	-nomoo:ntoo
England	injini	eenjee:nee
	iNgilandi	eengeela:ndee

English – Zulu

English	Zulu	
English (language)	isiNgisi	eeseengeːsee
to enjoy	-jabulela	-jaabooleːlaa
enjoy your meal!	ukujabulele ukudla!	oogoojaabooleːle oogooːtʒaa!
enough	-anele	-aaneːle
enquiry desk	ideski lokuthola ukwaziswa	eedeːskee lokutoːlaa ukwaaziːswaa
to enter	-ngena	-ngeːnaa
entrance	umnyango	oomnyaːːngo
entrance fee	imali yokungena	eemaaːlee yokoongeːnaa
equipment	amathuluzi	aamaatoolooːzee
equal	-lingene	-leengeːne
error	isiphosiso	eesposeːso
to escape	-sinda	-seeːndaa
essential	-funeka	-fooneːgaa
euro	i-euro	ee-euro
Europe	iYurophu	eeyooroːpoo
European	owaseYurophu	owaaseyoororooːpoo

English	Zulu	
evening	kusihlwa	koosiːʰwaa
this evening	namhlanje kusihlwa	naamdaaːnje koosee:ʰwaa
every	-nke	-nke
everyone	bonke	boːnke
everything	konke	koːnke
everywhere	zonke izindawo	zoːnke eezeendaaːwo
example: for example	ngokwesibonelo	ngoogwesboneːlo
excellent	-hle kakhulu	-ʰle kaakooːloo
exchange	ukwabelana	oogwaabelaaːnaa
exchange rate	izinga lokushintshiselana	eezeeːngaa lokooshi-ntsheeselaaːnaa
to exchange	-shintsha	-shee:nchaa
exciting	-thakazelisa	-taagaazeleeːsaa
excuse: excuse me! (to get by)	ngiyaxolisa!	ngeeyaa//oːlee:saa!
	ngiyaxolisa	ngeeyaa//oːlee:saa

exercise	-elula umzimba	-eloo:laa
exhibition	umbukiso	oomzee:mbaa
exit	indawo yokuphuma	oomboogee:so eendaa:wo
expenses	izindleko	yogoopoo:maa eezeentje:go
expensive	-mba eqolo	-mba e!ʔo:lo
to expire	-phelelwe yisikhathi	-pele:lwe yeeskaa:tee
to explain	-chaza	-/haa:zaa
to export	-davisa ezweni elingaphandle	ezwe:nee elee-ngaapaa:ntje
extra (more)	-ngaphezulu	-ngaapezoo:loo
eye	iso	ee:so
eyes	amehlo	aame:4o

F

| face | ubuso | ooboo:so |
| facilities | amalungiselelo | aamaaloo-ngeesele:lo |

to faint	-quleka	-lʔoole:gaa
fair (just)	-lungile	-loongee:le
fair (funfair)	i-funfair	eefunfair
fake	inkohliso	eenkoʔkee:so
fall	ukuwa	oogoo:waa
to fall	-wa	-waa
family	umndeni	oomnde:nee
famous	-dumile	-doomee:le
far	kude	koo:de
is it far?	kukude?	koogoo:de?
fare	imali	eemaa:lee
(bus, etc.)		
farm	yokugibela ipulazi	yogoogeebe:laa eeplaa:zee
fast	masinyane	maaseenyaa:ne
too fast	masinyane kakhulu	maaseenyaa:ne kaakoo:loo
to fasten (seatbelt)	-bopha	-bo:paa
fat (noun)	amafutha	aamaafoo:taa
father	ubaba	oobaa:baa

English - Zulu

English	Zulu	
father-in-law (father of husband)	ubabezala	oobaabezza:la
(father of wife)	umukhwe	oomoo:kwe
fault (defect)	iphutha	eepoo:taa
it's not my fault	akulona iphutha lami	aagoolo:naa eepoo:taa
favour	umusa	oomoo:saa
favourite	intandokazi	eentaandoo-gaa:zee
fax	isikhahlamezi	eeskaałaame:zee
by fax	ngesikhahlamezi	ngeskaałaa-me:zee
fax number	inombolo yesikhahlamezi	eenombo:lo yeskaałaamezee
to fax (document)	-thumela	-toome:laa
(person)	-thumela umuntu isikhahlamezi	-toome:laa oomoo:ntoo eeskaałaame:zee

English	Zulu	
February	ngoFebruwari	ngoFebroowaa:ree
to feel	-zwa	-zwaa
I feel sick	angizizwa kahle	aangeezee:zwaa kaa:łe
I don't feel well	angizizwa kahle	aangeezee:zwaa kaa:łe
feet	izinyawo	eezeenyaa:wo
female (human)	owesifazane	owesfaazaa:ne
(animal)	insikazi	eentseegaa:zee
fever	imfiva	eemfee:vaa
few	-mbalwa	-mbaa:lwaa
a few	-mbalwa	-mbaa:lwaa
fiancé(e)	insizwa	eentsee:zwaa
(fiancé)	ethembise	etembe:se
	intombi	eento:mbee
(fiancee)	ethembise	etembe:se
	insizwa	eentsee:zwaa
to fight	-lwa	-lwaa
to fill	-gcwalisa	-/gwaalee:saa
to fill in (form)	-gcwalisa	-/gwaalee:saa

English	Zulu	Pronunciation
film (movie, camera)	ifilimu	eefeelee:moo
to find	-thola	-to:laa
fine (penalty)	inhlawulo	een+aawoo:lo
finger	umunwe	oomoo:nwe
to finish	-qeda	-?e:daa
finished	-qedile	-?edee:le
fire	umlilo	oomlee:lo
fire alarm	umkhosi womlilo	oomko:see womlee:lo
fire escape (staircase)	indawo yokubalekela umlilo	eendaa:wo yogoobaalege:laa oomlee:lo
fire extinguisher	isicishamlilo	ees://eeshaa-mlee:lo
firm (company)	ifemu	eefe:moo
first	-okuqala	-ogoo?aa:laa
first aid	usizo lokuqala	oosee:zo logoo?aa:laa
first class	ufesikilasi	oofeeseekeelaa:see
first name	igama	eegaa:maa

English	Zulu	Pronunciation
fish	inhlanzi	een+aa:ndzee
to fish	-doba	-do:baa
fit (medical)	-qinile	-?eenee:le
to fit: *it doesn't fit me*	akungilingene	aagoongee-leenge:ne
to fix (repair)	-lungisa	-loongee:saa
can you fix it?	ungakulungisa?	oongaakoo-loongee:saa?
flat (apartment)	ifulethi	eefle:tee
flat (level)	-qondile	-?ondee:le
(beer)	-shodile	-shodee:le
flavour (of ice cream, etc.)	ukunambitheka	oogoonaa-mbeete:gaa
flesh	inyama	eenyaa:maa
flight	ibhanoyi	eebaano:yee
floor (of room)	iphansi	eepaa:ntsee
(storey)	isitezi	eeste:zee
(on the) **ground floor**	ngaphansi kwesitezi	ngaapaa:ntsee kweste:zee
(on the) **first floor**	esitezi sokuqala	este:zee so-goo?aa:laa

English – Zulu

English	Zulu	
flour	ufulawa	oofoolaa:waa
flower	imbali	eembaa:lee
flu	imfuluwenza	eemfooloo-we:ndzaa
to fly	-ndiza	-ndee:zaa
fog	inkungu	eenkoo:ngoo
to follow	-landela	-laande:laa
food	ukudla	oogoo:ɬaa
food poisoning	ubuthi obusekudleni	ooboo:tee oboo-segoo:be:nee
foot	unyawo	oonyaa:wo
to go on foot	-hamba ngezinyawo	-haa:mba ngezeenyaa:wo
footpath	indlela yezinyawo	eentɬe:laa yezeenyaa:wo
forbidden	-nqatshelwe	-nɬaache:lwe
foreign	-kwelinye izwe	-kwelee:nye ee:zwe
foreigner	owakwelinye izwe	owaakwelee:nye ee:zwe
forever	naphakade	naapaagaa:de

English	Zulu	
to forget	-khohlwa	-ko:4waa
fork (for eating)	imfologo	eemfolo:go
form (document)	ifomu	eefo:moo
(shape, style)	isimo	eesee:mo
fortnight	amasonto amabili	aamaaso:nto aamaabee:lee
forward	phambili	paambee:lee
fracture	ukuvaveka	oogoovaave:gaa
fragile	-phuka kalula	-poo:gaa kaaloo:laa
free (not occupied)	-ngasetshenziswa	-ngaasetshe-ndzee:swaa
free (costing nothing)	mahhala	maahaa:laa
freezer	isiqandisi	eesiʔaandee:see
frequent	ngokuphinda-phinda	ngoogoopeendaa-pee:ndaa
fresh	-sha	-shaa
Friday	ngoLwesihlanu	ngolwes4aa:noo
fried	-thosiwe	-tosee:we
friend	umngane	oomngaa:ne
friendly	-nomusa	-nomoo:saa

frog	ixoxo	ee//ʔoː/ʔo
from	*	
I'm from England	ngivela eNgilandi	ngeeve:laa eNgeelaːŋGee
I'm from Scotland	ngivela esiKotilandi	ngeeve:laa eskotllaa:ŋdee
front	phambili	paambee:lee
in front of...	*	
frost	ungqoqwane	oonǃgoǃwaaːne
frozen	-qandisiwe	-/ʔaaŋdeeseeːwe
fruit	izithelo	eezeeːlo
fruit juice	ujusi wezithelo	oojooːsee wezeeteːlo
to fry	-thosa	-toːsaa
fuel	uphethilomu	oopeteeloːmoo
full (e.g. hall)	-gcwele	-/ǃweːlee
full board	indawo yokula eendaːwo yogoolaaːlaa	

fun: to have fun	-zijabulisa	-zeejaabooːleeːsaa
funny (amusing)	-namahlaya	-naamaaǂaaːyaa
furnished	-nefenisha	-nefeneeːshaa
future	ikusasa	eegoosaaːsaa

G

gallery	igalari	eegalaːree
game (meat)	inyama	eenyaaːmaa
	yenyamazane	yenyaamaazaane
garage (petrol, repair)	igalaji	eegaalaaːjee
garden	ingadi	eengaaːdee
garlic	ugalikhi	oogaalee:kee
generous	-nokuphana	-nogoopaaːnaa
gents' (toilet)	amathoyilethi	aamaatoyeele:tee
	abesilisa	aabeseeleeːsaa
to get (obtain) (to fetch)	-thola	-toːlaa
	-landa	-laaːndaa
to get in (vehicle)	-ngena	-ngeːnaa
to get off (bus, etc)	-ehla	-eǂaa

English – Zulu

English	Zulu	Pronunciation
gift	isipho	eesee:po
gift shop	istolo sezipho	eesto:lo sezee:po
girl/girlfriend	intombi	eento:mbee
to give	-nika	-nee:gaa
to give back	-buyisa	-booyee:saa
glass	ingilazi	eengeelaa:zee
a glass of water	ingilazi yamanzi	eengeelaa:zee yaamaa:ndzee
glasses (spectacles)	izibuko	eezeeboo:go
gloves	amagilavu	aamaageelaa:voo
gluten	inomfi	eeno:mfee
to go (somewhere)	-ya	-yaa
(to leave)	-hamba	-haa:mbaa
I'm going to...	ngiya e...	ngee:yaa e...
(I intend to)	ngifuna uku...	ngeefoo:naa oogoo...
to go back	-buyela	-booyee:laa
to go in	-ngena	-nge:naa
to go out (leave)	-phuma	-poo:maa
good	kuhle	koo:4e
gram	igremu	egre:moo
grandchildren	abazukulwane	aabaazoo-goolwaa:ne
grandparents	umkhulu	oomkoo:loo
grape	igilebhisi	eegeelebee:see
greasy	-namafutha	-naamaafoo:taa
great (big)	-khulu	-koo:loo
great (wonderful)	-hle kakhulu	-4e kaakoo:loo
Great Britain	iNgilandi	eengeela:ndee
green	-luhlaza	-loo4aa:zaa
greengrocer's	istolo semifino nezithelo	eesto:lo semee-feeno nezeetelo
grey	-mpunga	-mpoo:ngaa
grilled	-thosiwe	-tosee:we
grocer's	istolo sokudla	eesto:lo sokoodla
ground floor (on the)	ngaphansi kwesitezi	ngaapaa:ntsee kweste:zee
group	isixuku	ees//'oo:goo
guest (in hotel, house)	isivakashi	eesvaagaa:shee
guesthouse	indlu yezivakashi	ee:ntgoo yezee-vaagaa:shee

English	Zulu	Pronunciation
guide (tourist guide)	umholi	oomhoʔi:lee
guidebook	incwadi yeziqondiso	een/waa:dee yezeeʔondee:so
guided tour	uhhambo oluqondiswayo	oohaa:mbo oloo-ʔondeeswaa.yo

H

English	Zulu	Pronunciation
hair	izinwele	eezeenwe:le
hairdresser	olungisa izinwele	oloongee:saa eezeenwe:le
hairdryer	isomisi zinwele	eesomee:see zeenwe:le
half	uhhafu	oohaa:foo
half an hour	uhhafu wehora	oohaa:foo weho:raa
half board	indawo yokulala nokudla kabili ngosuku	eendaa:wo yogoolaa:laa nogoo:ʤaa kaabee:lee ngosoo:goo

English	Zulu	Pronunciation
half-price	uhhafu wentengo	oohaa:foo wente:ngo
ham (cooked)	umlenze ophekiwe	oomle:nze opegee:we
(cured)	umlenze ogqunyisiwe	oomle:nze olgoonyeeseewe
hamburger	ibhega	eebe:gaa
hand	isandla	eesa:nʤaa
handbag	isikhwama	eeskwaa:maa
hand-made	enziwe ngezandla	-endzee:we ngezaa:nʤaa
handicapped	-khubazekile	-koobaazegee:le
handkerchief	iduku	eedoo:goo
handsome	-bukeka	-booge:gaa
hangover	ibhabhalazi	eebabbaalaa:zee
to happen	-enzeka	-endze:gaa
what happened?	kwenzekeni?	kwendzege:nee?
happy	-jabula	-jaaboo:laa
hard (not soft)	-lukhuni	-lookoo:nee

English	Zulu	Pronunciation
(not easy)	-nzima	-ndzee:maa
to have	-na-	-naa-
to have to	-fanele uku-	-faane:le oogoo-
hay fever	imfiva ethimulisayo	eemfee:vaa etee-mooleesaa:yo
he	u-	oo-
head	ikhanda	eekaa:ndaa
headache	-phethwe yikhanda	-pe:twe yeekaa:ndaa
I have a headache	ngiphethwe yikhanda	ngeepe:twe yeekaa:ndaa
health	impilo	eempee:lo
health food shop	isitolo sokudla okunempilo	eesto:lo sogoo:ʈaa ogoonempee:lo
healthy	-nempilo	-nempee:lo
to hear	-zwa	-zwa
heart	inhliziyo	eenhlee:zeeyo
heartburn	isilungulelo	eesloongoole:lo
heating	ukufudumeza	oogoofoo-doome:zaa

English	Zulu	Pronunciation
to heat up	-fudumeza	-foodoome:zaa
heavy	-sinda	-see:ndaa
height	ubude	ooboo:de
hello (on telephone)	sawubona	saawoobo:naa
helmet	umakalabha	oomaagaalaa:baa
help!	ngisize!	ngeesee:ze!
to help	-siza	-see:zaa
can you help me?	ungangisiza?	oongaangee-see:zaa?
her/his	-khe	-ke
her passport	iphasiphothi yakhe	eepaaseepoo:tee yaa:ke
her suitcases	amasutikesi akhe	aamaasootee-ke:see aa:ke
herbal tea	itiye lamakhambi	eetee:ye laamaakaa:mbee
here	lapha	laa:paa
here is/are...	*	*
hi!	sawubona!	saawoobo:naa!
high	-phakeme	-paage:me

English	Zulu	Pronunciation
him	yena	ye:naa
to hire	-qasha	-ı?aa:shaa
hired car	imoto eqashiwe	eemo:to eı?aashee:we
his passport	iphasiphothi yakhe	ibphasipho:tee yaa:ke
his suitcases	amasutikesi akhe	aamaasootee-ke:see aa:ke
historic	-nomlando	-nomlaa:ndo
hobby	isilibaziso	eesleebaazee:so
to hold (contain)	-qukatha	-ı?oogaa:taa
hold-up (in traffic)	ukubambeze-leka	oogoobaambeze-le:gaa
holiday	iholide	eeholee:de
on holiday	-seholideni	-seholeede:nee
home	ikhaya	eekaa:yaa
at my/your/our home	ekhaya lami, lakho, lethu	ekaa:yaa laa:mee, laa:ko, le:too
homosexual	inkonkoni	eenkonko:nee
honest	-qotho	-ı?o:to
to hope	-themba	-te:mbaa
I hope not	angithembi kanjalo	aangeete:mbee kaanjaa:lo
I hope so	ngithemba kanjalo	ngeete:mbaa kaanjaa:lo
hors d'oeuvre	izibiliboco zokuqala	eezeebeeleebo:/?o zogoo:ı?aa:laa
horse	ihhashi	eehaa:shee
hospital	isibhedlela	eesbetge:laa
hostel	ihostela	eehoste:laa
(youth hostel)	labasha	laabaa:shaa
hot	-shisa	-shee:saa
I'm hot	ngiyashisa	ngeeyaashee:saa
it's hot (weather)	kuyashisa	kooyaashee:saa
hotel	ihhotela	eehote:laa
hour	ihora	eeho:raa
half an hour	uhhafu wehora	oohaa:foo weho:raa
one hour	ihora elilodwa	eeho:raa eleelo:dwaa
house	indlu	ee:nɓoo

English – Zulu

house wine	iwayini lerestoranti	eewaayee:nee lerestoraa:ntee
how?	kanjani?	kaanjaa:nee?
how much?	kangakanani?	kaangaagaa-naa:nee?
how many?	-ngaki?	-ngaa:gee?
how are you?	unjani?	oonjaa:nee?
hungry: to be hungry	-lambile	-laambee:le
I'm hungry	ngilambile	ngeelaambee:le
hurry: I'm in a hurry	ngijahile	ngeejaahee:le
to hurt: to hurt somebody	-limaza	-leemaa:zaa
that hurts	kubuhlungu lokho	kooboo0oo:ngoo lo:ko
husband	umyeni	oomye:nee
hut (mountain)	iqhugwane	eel!hoogwaa:ne
I	ngi-	ngee-

ice (cube)	u-ayisi	ooaayee:see
with ice	u-ayisi	ooaayee:see
without ice	-ngena-ayisi	-noaayee:see -ngena-aayee:see
ice cream	u-ayisikhilimu	ooaayeesee-klee:moo
idea	umqondo	oom!?o:ndo
identity card	umazisi	oomaazee:see
if	uma	oo:maa
ill	-gula	-goo:laa
illness	isifo	eesee:fo
immediately	ngokushesha	ngogooshe:sha
to import	-ngenisa izimpahla zakwelinye izwe	-ngenee:saa eezeempaa:4aa zaagwelee:nyee ee:zwe
important	-balulekile	-baaloolegee:le
impossible	-ngenakwenzeka	-ngenaagwe-ndze:gaa
to improve	-thuthukisa	-tootoogee:saa
in	e...	e...

English	Zulu	
in two hours' time	emva kwamahora amabili	e:mvaa kwaamaaho:raa aamaabee:lee
in Canada	eKhanda	ekana:daa
in London	eLandani	elaanda:nee
in front of	*	*
included	-hlanganisiwe	-taangaanee-see:xe
to increase	-anda	-aa:ndaa
indigestion	ukuqumbelana	oogoo?'oombe-laa:naa
indoors	phakathi endlini	paagaa:tee engee:nee
infection	ukuhlaselwa yigciwane	oogoo4aase:lwaa yee-/geewaa:ne
information	ukwaziswa	oogwaazee:swaa eezeetaa:go
ingredients	izithako	
to injure	-limaza	-leemaa:zaa
injured	-limele	-leeme:le
insect	isinambuzane	eesnaa-mboozaa:ne

English	Zulu	
inside	phakathi	paagaa:tee
instant coffee	ikhofi elisheshayo	eeko:fee eleesheshaa:yoo
instead of	*	*
insurance	umshuwalense	oomshoo-waale:ntse
insurance certificate	istifiketi somshuwa-lense	eesteefeeke:tee somshoowaa-le:ntse
to insure	-vikela ngo-mshuwalense	-veege:laa ngo-mshoowaalentse
insured	-vikelwe ngo-mshuwalense	-veege:lwe ngo-mshoowaalentse
interesting	-thakazelisayo	-taagaaze-leesaa:yo
international	-ezizwe	-ezee:zwe
into	ngezizwe	ngezee:zwe
into town	ngaphakathi edolobheni	ngaapaagaa:tee edolobe:nee
to introduce	-ethula	-etoo:laa
invitation	isimemo	eesme:mo

English – Zulu

to invite	-mema	**jeweller's**	isitolo
invoice	i-invoyisi		samagugu
Ireland	i-Ayilendi		okuhloba
Irish	i-Ayirishi	**jewellery**	amajuweli
iron (for clothes)	i-ayini	**Jewish**	-ngumjuda
iron (metal)	insimbi	**job**	umsebenzi
is	*	**to join** (become member)	-joyina
island	isiqhingi		
it	ku-	**to joke**	-tekula
to itch	-luma	**journey**	uhambo
it itches	kuyaluma	**juice**	ujusi
		fruit juice	ujusi wezithelo
J			
jacket	ibhantshi	*orange juice*	ujusi
waterproof jacket	ibhantshi		wamawolintshi
January	lemvula	**July**	uJulayi
	uJanuwari	**to jump**	-eqa
jar (honey, jam etc.)	isitsha	**June**	uJuni
jeans	i-denim	**K**	
jellyfish	itheketheke	**to keep** (retain)	-gcina

	-me:maa		eesto:lo
	ee-eenvoyee:see		saamaagoo:goo
	eeaayeele:ndee		ogoolo:baa
	eeaayeeree:shee		aamaajoowe:lee
	eeaayee:nee		-ngoomjoo:daa
	eentsee:mbee		oomsebe:ndzee
	*		-joyee:naa
	eeslhee:ngee		
	koo-		-tegoo:laa
	-loo:maa		oohaa:mbo
	kooyaaloo:maa		oojoo:see
			oojoo:see
			wezeete:lo
	eebaa:nchee		oojoo:see waa-
	eebaa:nchee		maawolee:nchee
	lemvoo:laa		oojoolaa:yee
	oojaanoowaa:ree		-e:i?aa
	eesee:chaa		oojoo:nee
	eedenim		
	eetegete:ge		-/gee:naa

English	Zulu	Pronunciation
keep the change (command)	gcina ushintshi	/gee:naa ooshee:nchee
key	isikhiye	eeskee:ye
the car key	isikhiye semoto	eeskee:ye semo:to
kill	-bulala	-boolaa:laa
kilo(gram)	ikhilogremu	eekeeloogre:moo
kilometre	ikhilomitha	keekeelome:taa
kind (person)	-nomusa	nomoo:saa
(sort)	uhlobo	oo4o:bo
kiosk (news stand)	indlwanyana yokudayisela	eentgwaanyaanaa yogoodaayee-se:laa
(phone box)	indawo yokushaya ucingo	eendaa:wo yogooshaa:yaa oo/ee:ngo
to kiss	-anga	-aa:ngaa
kitchen	ikhishi	eekee:shee
knee	idolo	eedo:lo
knife	ummese	oome:se
to knock (on door)	-ngqongqoza	-nɟgonɟgo:zaa
to know	-azi	-aa:zee

English	Zulu	Pronunciation
I don't know	angazi	aangaa:zee
to know how to do sth	-yakwazi uku-	-yaagwaa:zee oogoo-
to know how to swim	-yakwazi ukubhukuda	-yaagwaa:zee oogooboo-goo:daa

L

English	Zulu	Pronunciation
ladies' (toilet)	amathoyilethi abesifazane	aamaatoyeele:tee abesfaazaa:ne
lady	intokazi	eentogaa:zee
lager	i-lager	eelager
lake	ichibi lemvelo	ee/hee:bee lemve:lo
lamb	izinyane	eezeenyaa:ne
to land	-ehla	-e:4aa
language	ulimi	oolee:mee
laptop	i-laptop	eelaptop
large	-khulu	-koo:loo
last	-gcina	-/gee:naa
last month	ngenyanga edlule	ngenyaa:ngaa etgoo:le

English – Zulu

English	Zulu		English	Zulu	
last night	ngobusuku obudlule	ngoboosoo:goo obootboo:le	(depart from)	-hamba	-haa:mbaa
last week	ngesonto eledlule	ngeso:nto eletgoo:le	(to leave behind)	-shiya	-shee:yaa
the last train	isitimela sokugcina	eesteeme:laa sogoo/gee:naa	to leave London	-shiya eLandani	-shee:yaa elaandaa:nee
late	-phuzile	-poozee:le	left: on/to the left	ngakweso-bunxele	ngaagweso-boon//e:ile
sorry we are late	siyaxolisa ngokufika sekwephuzile	seeyaa//?olee:saa ngogoofee:gaa segwepoozee:le	left-luggage (office)	ihhovisi lomthwalo oshiyiwe	eehovee:see lomtwaa:lo osheeyee:we
later	kamuva	kamoo:vaa	leg	umlenze	oomle:ndze
to laugh	-hleka	-te:gaa	lemon	ulamula	oolaamoo:laa
lavatory	ithoyilethi	eetoyeele:tee	lemonade	ulemoneti	oolemone:tee
laxative	umuthi woku-lambulula isisu	oomoo:tee wogoo-haa-mboolooo:laa	to lend	-boleka	-bole:gaa
to leak: it's leaking	kuyavuza	eesee:soo kooyaavoo:zaa	length	ubude	ooboo:de
to learn	-funda	-foo:ndaa	lens (of camera, etc.)	ilensi	eele:ntsee
to leave (depart)	-ya	-yaa	lens (contact lens)	i-contact lense	eecontact lense
			lesbian	isitabani	eestaabaa:nee
			less	-ncanyana	-n//aanyaa:naa
			less than	*	
			to let (allow)	-vumela	-voome:laa

English	Zulu	Pronunciation
(to hire out)	-qashisa	-'paashee:saa
letter	incwadi	een/waa-dee
licence	ilayisense	eelaayeese:ntse
to lie down	-lala phansi	-laa:laa paa:ntsee
life jacket	ijazi lokuntanta	eejaa:zee logoontaa:ntaa
lift (elevator)	ilifti	eelee:ftee
light	isibani	eesbaa:nee
have you got a light?	unayo ilayitha?	oonaa:yo eelaayee:taa?
like (preposition)	-lula	-loo:laa
like this	njenga-njengalokhu	njengaa-njengaalo:koo
to like	-thanda	-taa:ndaa
I don't like coffee	angilithandi ikhofi	aangeeleetaa:-ndee eeko:fee
I like coffee	ngithanda ikhofi	ngeetaa:ndaa eeko:fee
I'd like...	ngingathanda...	ngeengaataa:-ndaa...

English	Zulu	Pronunciation
we'd like...	singathanda...	seengaataa:-ndaa...
line (mark, queue)	umugga	oomoo:(g)gaa
line (telephone)	intambo	eentaa:mbo
liqueur	izinyembezi zikakhwini	eezeenyembe:zee zeegaakwee:nee
list	uhlu	oo:4oo
to listen to	-lalela	-laale:laa
little	-litha	eelee:ta
little	-ncane	-'nj/aa:ne
to live (in a place)	-hlala	-4aa:laa
I live in London	ngihlala eLandani	ngee4aa:laa elaandaa:nee
to lock	-khiya	-kee:yaa
London	iLandani	eelaandaa:nee
to/in London	eLandani	elaandaa:nee
long	-de	-de
for a long time	isikhathi eside	eeskaatee eseede
to look after	-nakekela	-naagege:laa
to look at	-buka	-boo:gaa
to look for	-funa	-foo:naa

English - Zulu

English – Zulu

English	Zulu	
loose (not fastened)	-xega	-/ʔe:gaa
to lose	-lahlekelwa	-laatege:lwaa
lost (object)	-lahlekelwe	-laatege:lwe
I've lost...	*	
I'm lost	ngidukile	ngeedoogee:le
lost property office	ihhovisi lezinto ezilahlekile	eehovee:see lezee:nto ezelaatege:le
lot: *a lot of*	-ningi	-nee:ngee
loud	-nomsindo	-nomsee:ndo
lounge	ilawungi	eelaawoo:njee
love	uthando	ootaa:ndo
to love	-thanda	-taa:ndaa
I love you	ngiyakuthanda	ngeeyaagoo-taa:ndaa
(food, activity, etc.) **I love**	ngithanda...	ngeetaa:ndaa...
I love swimming	ngithanda ukubhukuda	ngeetaa:ndaa oogoobooboo:daa
lovely	-hle	-e
low	-phansi	-paa:ntsee
low tide	ibuya elishile	eeboo:yaa eleeshee:le
luck	inhlanhla	eenɬaa:nɬaa
lucky	-nenhlanhla	-nenɬaa:nɬaa
luggage	umthwalo	oomtwaa:lo
luggage trolley	ingola yomthwalo	eenjo:laa yomtwaa:lo
lunch	ilantshi	eelaa:nchee
M		
machine	umshini	oomshee:nee
magazine	umagazini	oomagazee:nee
mail	iposi	eepo:see
by mail	ngeposi	ngepo:see
main	-khulu	-koo:loo
main course (of meal)	isidlo esikhulu	eesee:tɡo eseekoo:loo
to make	-enza	-e:ndzaa
make-up	ukuzincwala	oogoozee-ŋ/waa:laa

English	Zulu	Pronunciation
male (person)	owesilisa	oweseelee:saa
man	indoda	eendo:daa
to manage (to be in charge of)	-phatha	-paa:taa
manager	umphathi	oompaa:tee
many	-ningi	-nee-ngee
map	ibalazwe	eebaalaa:zwe
road map	ibalazwe lemigwaqo	eebaalaa:zwe lemeegwaa:i?o
street map	ibalazwe lezitaladi	eebaalaa:zwe lezeetaalaa:dee
March	uMashi	ooMaa:shee
margarine	umajarini	oomaajaaree:nee
market	imakethe	eemaake:te
where is the market?	imakethe ikuphi?	eemaake:te eegoo:pee?
marmalade	imamaledi	eemaamaale:dee
married	-shadile	-shaadee:le
I'm married	ngishadile	ngeeshaadee:le
mass (in church)	imisa	eemee:saa
match (sport)	imeshi	eeme:shee
matches	umentshisi	oomenchee:see
to matter: it doesn't matter	akunandaba	agoonaandaa:baa
what's the matter?	kwenzekani?	kwendzegaa:nee?
May	uMeyi	oome:yee
mayonnaise	imayonezi	eemayone:zee
me	-ngi-	-ngee-
meal	ukudla	oogoo:ʣaa
to mean	-sho	-sho
what does this mean?	kusho ukuthini lokhu?	koo:sho oogootee:nee lo:koo?
meat	inyama	eenyaa:maa
medicine	umuthi	oomoo:tee
to meet	-hlangana	-haangaa:naa
meeting	umhlangano	oomhlaangaa:no
memory	inkumbulo	eenkoomboo:lo
men	amadoda	aamaado:daa
to mend	-lungisa	-loongee:saa
menu	imenu	eemenu

English – Zulu

message	umyalezo	**with milk/**	-nobisi
meter/metre	imitha	**without milk**	-ngenabisi
midday	imini	**millimetre**	imilimitha
at midday	emini	**to mind: do you**	nginga...?
middle	phakathi	**mind if I...?**	
midnight	phakathi kwamabili	**I don't mind**	anginandaba nginga...?
at midnight	phakathi kwamabili	**do you mind?**	amanzi
mild (weather, cheese)	-pholile	**mineral water**	esiphethu
		minimum	okuncane kakhulu
milk	ubisi	**minute**	iminithi
milk (curry)	ubisi		*
baby milk (formula)	lomntwana	**minute**	
fresh milk	ubisi olusha	**to miss** (train, flight, etc.)	
		Miss (when addressing)	Nkosazana
powdered milk	ubisi olu-yimpuphu	**missing** (disappeared)	-lahlekile
soya milk	ubisi lukasoya	**mistake**	iphutha
		to mix	-xuba

oomyaale:zo	-nobee:see
eemee:taa	-ngenaabee:see
eemee:nee	eemeeleemee:taa
eme:nee	ngeenga...?
paagaa:tee	
paagaa:tee kwamaabee:lee	angeenaandaabaa ngeenga...?
paagaa:tee kwamaabee:lee	aamaa:ndzee
-polee:le	espe:too
	ogoon/aa:ne
	kaakoo:loo
-ngaabaa:bee	eemeenee:tee
oobee:see	
oobee:see	
lomntwaa:naa	nkosaazaa:naa
oobee:see	
oloo:shaa	
oobee:see oloo-yeempoo:poo	-laa+egee:le
oobee:see	
loogaaso:yaa	eepoo:taa
	-//?oo:baa

English	Zulu	Pronunciation
mobile (phone)	umakhalekhukhwini	oomaakaalekoo-kwee:nee
mobile number	inombolo kamakhalekhukhwini	enombo:lo kaamaakaale-kookwee:nee
moment: at the moment	okwamanje	ogwaamaa:nje
Monday	uMsombuluko	oomsombooloogo
money	imali	eemaa:lee
I have no money	anginayo imali	aangeenaa:yo eemaa:lee
this month	inyanga ngale nyanga	eenyaa:ngaa ngaa:le nyaa:ngaa
next month	ngenyanga ezayo	ngenyaa:ngaa ezaa:yo
moon	inyanga	eenyaa:ngaa
more	-nye	-nye
more wine	elinye iwayini	elee:nye eewaayee:nee
more than	*	*
more than three	ngaphezu kokuthathu	ngaape:zoo kogootaa:too
morning	ukusa	oogoo:saa
in the morning	ekuseni	egoose:nee
tomorrow morning	kusasa ekuseni	koosaa:saa egoose:nee
mosquito	umiyane	oomeeyaa:ne
mosquito net	inethi likamiyane	eene:tee leegaameeyaa:ne
most (of the)	*	*
mother	umama	ooma:maa
mother-in-law (mother of husband)	umamezala	oomaamezaa:laa
(mother of wife)	umkhwekazi	oomkwega:zee
motor	imotho	eemo:to
motorbike	isithuthuthu	eestootoo:too
motorboat	isikebhe esinenjini	eeske:be eseenenjee:nee
motorway	umgwaqo omkhulu	oomgwaa:i?o omkoo:loo

English – Zulu

mountain	intaba	eentaa:baa
mouth	umlomo	oomlo:mo
to move	-nyakaza	-nyaaga:zaa
it's moving	kuyanyakaza	kooyaanyaa-gaa:zaa
movie	ifilimu	eefeelee:moo
Mr (when addressing)	Mnumzane	mnoomzaa:ne
Mrs/Ms	Nkosikazi	nkoseegaa:zee
much	-ningi	-nee:ngee
too much	-ningi kakhulu	-nee:ngee kakoo:loo
muddy	-nodaka	-nodaa:gaa
to mug; I've been mugged	ngiphangiwe	ngeepaangee:we
muscle	umsipha	oomsee:paa
museum	imnyuziyemu	eemnyuoozee-ye:moo
music	umculo	oom/?oo:lo
must	-fanele	-faane:le
my	-mi	-mee

my passport	iphasiphothi yami	eepaaseepo:tee yaa:mee
my room	ikamelo lami	eekaame:lo laa:mee
my suitcases	amasutikesi ami	aamaasootee-ke:see aa:mee
N		
name	igama	eega:maa
my name is...	igama lami ngu...	eegaa:maa laa:mee ngoo...
what is your name?	ungubani igama lakho?	oongoobaa:nee eegaa:maa laa:ko?
narrow	-mngcingo	-mnj/gee:ngo
national	-kazwelonke	-kaazwelo:nke
nationality	isizwe	eesee:zwe
natural	-kwemvelo	-kwemve:lo
near	*	
is it near?	kuseduze?	koosedoo:ze?
near the bank	eduze nebhange	edoo:ze nebaa:nge

English	Zulu	Pronunciation
to need (to)	-dinga	-dee:ngaa
I need...	ngidinga...	ngeedee:ngaa...
we need...	sidinga...	seedee:ngaa...
I need to	kudingeka	koodeenge:gaa
phone	ngishaye ucingo	ngeeshaa:ye oo/?ee:ngo
never	ngeke	nge:ge
new	-sha	-shaa
news	izindaba	eezeendaa:baa
newspaper	iphephandaba	eepepaandaa:baa
news stand	indawo yokuthengisa amabhuku	eendaa:wo yogootengge:saa aamaaboo:goo
New Year	uNyaka omusha	oonyaa:gaa omo:shaa
happy New Year!	uNyaka omusha omuhle!	oonyaa:gaa omo:shaa omo:4e!
New Zealand	iNyuzilandi	enyoozeela:ndee
next (in time phrases)	-zayo	-zaa:yo
(after)	-landelayo	-laandelaa:yo
next Monday	ngoMsombuluko ozayo	ngomsomboo-loo:go ozaa:yo
next to	*	
next week	ngesonto elizayo	ngeso:nto eleezaa:yo
the next train	isitimela esilandelayo	eesteeme:laa eseelaandelaa:yo
nice (enjoyable)	-hle -mnandi	-4e -mnaa:ndee
nice (person)	-hle	-4e
niece	umshanakazi	oomshaa-naagaa:zee
night (night-time)	ubusuku	ooboosoo:goo
night (evening)	kusihlwa	koosee:4waa
at night	ebusuku	eboosoo:goo
last night	izolo ebusuku	eezo:lo eboosoo:goo
tomorrow night (evening)	kusasa ebusuku (kusihlwa)	koosaa:saa eboosoo:goo (koosee:4waa)

English – Zulu

English – Zulu

English	Zulu	Pronunciation
tonight	namhlanje ebusuku	naam4aa:nje eboosoo:goo
nightclub	indawo yoku-zithokozisa ebusuku	eenda:awo yogoo-zeetogozee:saa eboosoo:goo
no (without)	cha	/haa
no problem	ayikho inkinga	aayee:ko eenkee:ngaa
no thanks	cha ngiyabonga	/haa ngeeyaabo:ngaa
nobody	*	*
noise	umsindo	oomsee:ndo
it's very noisy	kunomsindo omkhulu	koonomsee:ndo omkoo:lo
non-alcoholic	-ngenasidaki	-ngenaasdaa:gee
none	lutho	loo:to
non-smoking (seat, compartment)	akubhenywa	aagoobe:nywaa
north	inyakatho	eenyagaa:to

English	Zulu	Pronunciation
Northern Ireland	i-Northern Ireland	eenorthern ireland
nose	ikhala	eekaa:laa
I am not...	angi...	aangee...
note (banknote)	imali eyiphepha	eemaa:lee eyeepe:paa
nothing	lutho	loo:to
nothing else (warning)	lutho olunye	loo:to oloo:nye
notice (sign)	isaziso	eesaazee:so
novel	imbiko	eembee:go
November	inoveli	eenove:lee
now	uNovemba	oonove:mbaa
nowhere	manje	maa:nje
number (quantity)	*	
(of room, house)	isibalo	eesbaa:lo
nut (to eat)	inombolo	eenombo:lo
	inathi	eenaa:tee
O		
ocean	ulwandle	oolwaa:n4e
October	u-Okthoba	oo-Okto:baa

English	Zulu	
odd (strange)	-mangalisayo	-maangaalee-saa:yo
of	*	
a glass of...	*	
made of...	*	
off (light)	-cishile	-ʔeeshee:le
(rotten)	-bolile	-bolee:le
office	ihhovisi	eehovee:see
often	kaningi	kaanee:ngee
oil (for car)	uwoyela	oowoye:laa
(for food)	amafutha	aamaafoo:taa
OK (agreed)	kulungile	kooloongee:le
(good)	hle	ɬe
old	-dala	-daa:laa
how old are you?	uneminyaka emingaki?	oonemeenyaagaa eemeengaa:gee?
I'm ... years old	ngineminyaka engu-...	ngeeneemeenyaa-gaa engoo....
on (light)	-khanya	-kaa:nyaa
(engine, etc.)	-sebenza	-sebe:ndzaa
on the table	etafuleni	etaafoole:nee

English	Zulu	
on time	ngesikhathi	ngeskaa:tee
once	kanye	kaa:nye
at once	ngokushesha	ngogooshe:shaa
onion	u-anyanisi	ooaanyaanee:see
only	kuphela	koope:laa
open	-vuliwe	-voolee:we
to open	-vula	-voo:laa
opposite the bank	*	
	malungana nebhange	maaloongaa:naa nebaa:nge
or	noma	no:maa
orange (fruit)	iwolintshi	eewolee:nchee
(colour)	-sawolintshi	-saawolee:nchee
orange juice	ujusi wamawolintshi	oojoo:see waa-maawolee:nchee
order (in restaurant)	i-oda	eeo:daa
out of order	*	
to order (in restaurant)	-oda	-o:daa

English – Zulu

English	Zulu		English	Zulu
organic	-kwezinto eziphilayo -kwezee:nto ezeepeelaa:yo		to overtake (in car)	-dlula -dlula
to organize	-hlela -ɬe:la		to owe	-kweleta -kwele:taa
other	-nye -nye		you owe me...	uyangikweleta... ooyaangee-kwele:taa...
have you	kukhona okunye kooko:naa ogoo:nye		**P**	
any others?	onakho? onaa:ko		to pack (luggage)	-pakisha impahla -paagee:shaa eempaa:ɬaa
our	-ithu -ee:too		package	uhambo oohaa:mbo
our room	ikamelo lethu eekaame:lo le:too		package tour	oluhlanganisa zonke izindleko oloo+aangaa-nee:saa zo:nke eezeenɟe:go
our baggage	umthwalo wethu oomntwaa:lo we:too			
out (light)	-cishe -/?eeshee:le		page	ikhasi eeka:si
he's/she's out	uphumile oopoome:le		paid	-khokhiwe -kokee:we
outside	phandle paa:nɟe		I've paid	ngikhokhile ngeekokee:le
over (on top of)	*		pain	ubuhlungu ooboo+oo:ngoo
to overbook	-bhukela ngokweqile -booge:laa ngogwe/?ee:le		painful	-buhlungu -boo+oo:ngoo
to overcharge	-biza imali eyeqileyo -bee:zaa eemaa:lee eye/?eele:yo		painkiller	isibulalazi-nhlungu eesboolaalaazee-n+oo:ngoo
			pair	ibhangqa eebaa:nɟgaa
			pale	-phaphathekile -paapaategee:le

English	Zulu	Pronunciation
pants (underwear)	ibhulukwe langaphansi	eebooloo:gwe laangaapaantsee
(trousers)	ibhulukwe	eebooloo:gwe
paper	iphepha	eepe:paa
parcel	iphasela	eepaase:laa
pardon? (please repeat)	ngicela uphinde	ngee/ʔe:laa oopee:nde
parents	abazali	aabaazaa:lee
park	ipaki	eepaa:gee
to park	-paka	-paa:gaa
part: *spare parts*	izipele	eezeepe:le
partner (business)	umlingani	oomleengaa:nee
(boyfriend)	isoka	eeso:gaa
(girlfriend)	intombi	eento:mbee
(cohabiting)	umasihlalisane	oomaasee-ɬaaleesaa:ne
party (group)	isixuku	ees/ʔoo:goo
(celebration)	umcimbi	oom/ʔe:mbee
(political)	iqembu	eelʔe:mboo
pass (bus, train)	ipasi	eepaa:see

English	Zulu	Pronunciation
(mountain)	isikhala sentaba	eeskaa:laa sentaa:baa
passenger	umgibeli	oomgeebe:lee
passport	iphasiphothi	eepaaseepo:tee
pasta	iphasta	eepaa:staa
path	umgudu	oomgoo:doo
to pay	-khokha	-ko:kaa
I'd like to pay	ngingathanda ukukhokha	ngeengaataandaa oogooko:kaa
where do I pay?	kufanele ngikhokhe kuphi?	koofaane:le ngeeko:ke koo:pee?
payment	inkokhelo	eenkoke:lo
payphone	isigxobo socingo	ees/ʔgo:bo so/ʔee:ngo
peach	ipetshisi	eepeetshi:see
peanut	intongomane	eentongomaa:ne
peanut allergy	i-aleji	eeale:je
pear	yamanathi iganandoda	yaamaanaa:tee eegaanaando:daa
peas	uphizi	oopee:zee

English – Zulu

English	Zulu		English	Zulu
to peel (fruit)	-/'we:/'waa		**pet**	isilwane	eeseelwaa:ne
pen	ipeni	eepe:nee			esifuywayo	eesefooywaa:yo
pensioner	umuntu ohola	oomoo:ntoo		**petrol**	uphetilomu	oopeteelo:moo
	impesheni	oho:laa		*unleaded*	i-unleaded	eeunleaded
		eempeshe:nee		*petrol station*	igalaji	eegaalaa:jee
people	abantu	aabaa:ntoo		**pharmacy**	ikhemisi	eekeme:see
pepper (spice)	upelepele	oopelepe:le		**phone**	ucingo	oo/'ee:ngo
pepper (vegetable)	uphepha	oope:paa		*by phone*	ngocingo	ngo/'ee:ngo
per	*			*phone box*	indawo	eendaa:wo
per day	ngosuku	ngoso:goo			yokushaya	yogooshaa:yaa
per hour	ngehora	ngeho:raa			ucingo	oo/'ee:ngo
per person	ngomuntu	oomoo:ntoo		*phone card*	ikhadi	eekaa:dee
					lokushaya	logooshaa:yaa
per week	ngamunye	ngaamoo:nye			ucingo	oo/'ee:ngo
	ngesonto	ngeso:nto		**to phone**	-shaya ucingo	-shaa:yaa
perfect	-phelele	-pele:le				oo/'ee:ngo
performance (show)	umbukiso	oomboogee:so		**to photocopy**	-enza	-e:ndzaa
					ifothokhophi	eefotoko:pee
perhaps	mhlawumbe	m4aawoo:mbe		**photograph**	isithombe	eesto:mbe
period (menstruation)	-sesikhathini	-seseekaatee:nee		*to take a*	-thatha	-taa:taa
person	umuntu	oomoo:ntoo		*photograph*	isithombe	eesto:mbe

English	Zulu	Pronunciation
phrasebook	incwadi yamabinzana	een/waa:dee yaamaabee-ndzaa:naa
to pick (choose)	-khetha	-ke:taa
(pluck)	-nqunta	-nʲoo:ntaa
picture (painting)	umdwebo	oomdwe:bo
(photo)	isithombe	eesto:mbe
pie (savoury)	uphayi	oopaa:yee
piece	ucezu	oo/?e:zoo
pier	insika yamatshe	eentsee:gaa yaamaa:che
pillow	umqamelo	oom?aame:lo
pink	-bomvana	-bomvaa:naa
pitch (place for tent)	indawo yokugxumeka itende	eendaa:wo yogoo-//goo-megaa eeten:de
(place for caravan)	ikharavani	eekarava:nee
(sport)	inkundla	eenkoo:nʤaa
pizza	i-pizza	eepizza
place	indawo	eendaa:wo
place of birth	indawo yokuzalwa	eendaa:wo yogoozaa:lwaa
plain (unflavoured)	-nakuna-mbitheka	-naagoona-mbeete:gaa
to plan	-lungiselela	-loongeesele:laa
plan (map)	ibalazwe	eebaalaa:zwe
plane (aircraft)	ibhanoyi	eebaano:yee
plastic (made of)	ngepulastiki	ngeplaastee:kee
plate	ipuleti	eeple:tee
platform (railway)	ipulatifomu	eepoolateefo:moo
which platform?	kuliphi ipulatifomu?	koolee:pee eepoola-teefo:moo?
play (at theatre)	umdlalo	oomʤaa:lo
to play (games)	-dlala	-ʤaa:la
pleasant	-mnandi	-mnaa:ndee
please	-cela	-/?e:laa
pleased	jabula	-jaaboo:laa
pleased to meet you	ngijabulela ukukwazi	ngeejaaboole:laa oogoogwaa:zee

English – Zulu

English	Zulu		English	Zulu
to plug in	-xhuma	-//hoo:maa	postbox	ibhokisi leposi	eebogee:see
plum	ipulamu	eepoolaa:moo	postcard	iphosikhadi	lepo:see
p.m.	pm	pm	postcode	ikhodi yeposi	eeposeekaa:dee
pocket	isikhwama	eeskwaa:maa			eeko:dee
poisonous	-noshevu	-noshe:voo	post office	iposi	yepo:see
police (force)	amaphoyisa	aamaapoyee:saa	to postpone	-hlehlisa	eepo:see
police station	isiteshi	eeste:shee	potato	izambane	-4e4ee:saa
polluted	samaphoyisa	saamaapoyeesaa	pound (weight)	iphawundi	eezaambaa:ne
pool (swimming)	-ngcolisiwe	-nj'goleesee:we	(money)	upondo	eepaawoo:ndee
	idamu	eedaa:moo	power (electricity)	ugesi	oopo:ndo
poor	lokubhukuda	logooboogoodaa	to prefer	-khetha	ooge:see
	-mpofu	-mpo:foo	pregnant	-khulelwe	-ke:taa
pork	inyama	eenya:maa	I'm pregnant	ngikhulelwe	-koole:lwe
	yengulube	yengooloo:be	to prepare	-lungiselela	ngeekoole:lwe
port (seaport)	itheku	eete:goo	prescription	incwadi	-loongeesele:laa
porter (for luggage)	umlindi	oomlee:ndee		yemithi	een/waa:dee
				kadokotela	yemee:tee
possible	-ngenzeka	-ngendze:gaa	present (gift)	isipho	kaadogote:laa
post (letters)	iposi	eepo:see	pretty	-hle	eesee:po
by post	ngeposi	ngepo:see	price	inani	-+e
to post	-posa	-po:saa			eenaa:nee

English	Zulu	Pronunciation
price list	uhlu lwamanani	oo:loo lwaamaanaa:nee
private	-ngasese	-ngaase:se
probably	-ngokunokwe-nzeka	-ngogoonogwe-ndze:gaa
problem	inkinga	eenkee:ngaa
prohibited	-ngatshelwe	-n'taache:lwe
to promise	isithembiso -thembisa	eestembee:so -tembee:saa
promise	-thana	-taa:naa
to pronounce	liphinyiswa	leepeenye:swaa
how's it pronounced?	kanjani?	kaanjaa:nee?
public	umphakathi	oompaagaa:tee
public holiday	iholide lomphakathi	eeholee:de lompaagaa:tee
to pull	-donsa	-do:nsaa
pullover	ijezi	eeje:zee
puncture	iphantshi	eepaa:nchee
purse	isikhwama semali	eeskwaa:maa semaa:lee
to push	-sunduza	-soondoo:zaa
pushchair	ikalishi lengane	eekaalee:shee lengaa:ne
to put (place)	-beka	-be:gaa
pyjamas	amaphijama	aamaapee-jaa:maa

Q

English	Zulu	Pronunciation
quality	ikhwalithi	eekhwaalee:tee
quantity	ubuningi	ooboonee:ngee
to quarrel	-xabana	-//?aabaa:naa
quarter	ikwata	eekwaa:taa
quay	iphoyinti	eepoyee:ntee
question	umbuzo	oomboo:zo
queue	umugqa	oomoo:!gaa
to queue	-hlaba uhele	-ɬaa:baa oohe:le
quick	ngokushesha	ngogooshe:shaa
quickly	masinyane	maaseenyaa:ne
quiet (place)	-thulile	-toolee:le
quiet (rather)	-ngcono	-n'go:no
quite (completely)	impela	eempe:laa
quite good	-hle kancane	-ɬe kaanj/aa:ne

English – Zulu

English – Zulu

R		
race (people)	uhlanga	ooɬaa:ngaa
(sport)	umjaho	oomjaa:ho
radio	umsakazo	oomsaagaa:zo
railway	ujoliwe	oololee:we
railway station	isiteshi	eeste:shee
rain	sikaloliwe	seegaalolee:we
to rain:	imvula	eemvoo:laa
it's raining	liyana	leeyaa:naa
raincoat	ijazi lemvula	eejaa:zee lemvoo:laa
raped:		
to be raped	-dlwengulwa	-ɬwengoo:lwaa
rare (uncommon)	-ngavamile	-ngaavaamee:le
(steak)	-vuthwe	-voo:twe
rash (skin)	kancane	kaanʒ/aa:ne
rate (price)	ukuqubuka	oogooʃooboogaa
	inani	eenaa:nee

rate of exchange	izinga lokushintshiselana	eezee:ngaa loogooshee-ncheeselaa:naa
raw	-vuthiwe	-vootee:we
razor	insingo	eentsee:ngo
razor blades	izinsingo	eezeentsee:ngo
to read	-funda	-foo:ndaa
ready	-lungele	-loonge:le
real	-ngempela	-ngempe:laa
to realize	-bona	-bo:naa
reception	ihhovisi	eehovee:see
(desk)	lokwamukela	logwaamoogeːlaa
receptionist	izihambi	eezeehaːmbee
recipe	umbambi	oombaa:mbee
	zingcingo	zeen/gee:ngo
	indlela	eenʃe:laa
to recognize	yokupheka	yogoope:gaa
to recommend	-khumbula	-koomboo:laa
red	-tusa	-too:saa
to reduce	-bomvu	-bo:mvoo
	-nciphisa	-n/eepee:saa

	English	Zulu	
eesaapoole:lo	reduction	isaphulelo	
oogoo-/gwaa-lee:saa	refill	ukugcwalisa	
-booyeese:laa	to refund	-buyisela imali	
eemaa:lee	to refuse	-ala	
-aa:laa	region	isifunda	
eesfoo:ndaa	register	incwadi yokubhalisa	
een/waa:dee yogoobaalee:saa	registered (letter)	-bhalisiwe	
-baaleese:we			
eefo:moo yo-goobaalee:saa	registration form	ifomu yokubhalisa	
-booyeese:laa	to reimburse	-buyisela	
ees:lo:bo	relation (family)	isihlobo	
ooboo4o:bo	relationship	ubuhlobo	
-koomboo:laa angeekoo-mboo:lee	remember	-khumbula angikhumbuli	
	I don't remember		
-soo:saa	to remove	-susa	

	English	Zulu	
eemaa:lee yogoote:laa	rental	imali yokuthela	
oogooloo-ngee:saa	repair	ukulungisa	
-loongee:saa	to repair	-lungisa	
-pee:ndaa	to repeat	-phinda	
-pendo:laa	to reply	-phendula	
oombee:go	report (of theft, etc.)	umbiko	
-bee:gaa	to report (theft, etc.)	-bika	
ees/?e:lo	request	isicelo	
-/?e:laa	to request	-cela	
oogooboo:gaa	reservation	ukubhuka	
-boo:gaa	to reserve	-bhuka	
-boogee:we	reserved	-bhukiwe	
eendaa:wo yeholee:de	resort (holiday)	indawo yeholide	
oogoopoomoolaa ogoosele:yo	rest (relaxation) (remainder)	ukuphumula okuseleyo	
-poomoo:laa	to rest	-phumula	

English – Zulu

English – Zulu

English	Zulu	Pronunciation
restaurant	isitolo sokudlela	eesto:lo sogoobje:laa
restaurant car	inqola yokudlela	eenjo:laa yogoobje:laa
retired	-thathe umhlalaphansi	-taa:te oomhaalaapaa:ntsee
to return (to a place)	-buyela	-booye:laa
to return (something)	-buyisa	-booye:saa
return ticket	iritheni / irayisi	eereete:nee / eeraayee:see
rich (person)	-cebile	-/'ebee:le
rich (food)	isibilebile	eesbeeleebee:le
to ride (horse)	-gibela ihhashi	-geebe:laa eehaa:shee
right (correct)	-nembile	-nembee:le
right: on/to the right	ngakwesokudla	ngaagweso goo:Jgaa
ring (on finger)	indandatho	eendaandaa:to

English	Zulu	Pronunciation
to ring (bell)	-shaya insimbi	-shaa:yaa eentsee:mbee
it's ringing (phone)	ucingo luyakhala	oo/'ee:ngo looyaakaa:laa
to ring somebody	-shayela ucingo	-shayela ucingo oo/'ee:ngo
river	umfula	oomfoo:laa
road	umgwaqo	oomgwaa:i?o
road map	ibalazwe	eebaalaa:zwe
road sign	lemigwaqo / uphawu	lemeegwaa:i?o / oopaa:woo
roast	inyama eyosiwe	eenyaa:maa eyosee:we
roll (bread)	ibhanisi	eebaanee:see
room (in house/hotel) (space)	ikamelo	eekaame:lo
double room	indawo / ikamelo / eliyidabuli	eendaa:wo / ekaame:lo / eleeeye-daaboo:lee

English	Zulu	Pronunciation
family room	ikamelo lomndeni wonke	eekaame:lo lomnde:nee wo:nke
single room	ikamelo eliyisingili	eekaame:lo eleeyee-seengee:lee
room number	inombolo yekamelo	eenombo:lo yekaame:lo
room service	isevisi yokulethelwa ukudla ehhotela	eesevee:see yogoolete:lwaa oogoo:tɣaa ehote:laa
rose	irozi	eero:zee
rosé wine	i-rosé	eerosé
rough:	ulwandle olunesivunguvungu	oolwaa:nʤe ooloonesivoo-ngoovoo:ngoo
rough sea	-yindilingi	-yeendee-lee:ngee
round	uhele	oohe:le
row (theatre, etc.)	izibi	eezee:bee
rubbish		
ruins	incithakalo	een/eetaagaa:lo
to run	-gijima	-geejee:maa
S		
sad	-dabukile	-daaboogee:le
safe (for valuables)	isisefo	eeseese:fo
safe	-phephile	-pepee:le
is it safe?	kuphephile?	koopepee:le?
sailing (sport)	ukuntweza	oogoontwe:zaa
salad	isaladi	eesaalaa:dee
salad dressing	isithokelo sesaladi	eestoge:lo sesaalaa:dee
sales (reductions)	izaphulelo	eezaapoole:lo
salesman/ woman	umthengisi	oomtengee:see
salt	usawoti	oosaawo:tee
salty	-nosawoti	-nosaawo:tee
same	-fanayo	-faanaa:yo
sand	isihlabathi	ees4aabaa:tee
sandwich	isemeshi	eeseme:shee

English - Zulu

English	Zulu	Pronunciation
satellite dish	indishi yesathelayithi	eendee:shee yesatelaayee:tee
satellite TV	i-TV elisebenza ngesathe-layithi	eetv eleeseebe:-ndzaa ngesate-laayee:tee
Saturday	uMgqibelo	oom!geebe:lo
sauce	isosi	eeso:see
sausage	isoseji	eesose:jee
to save (life)	-sindisa	-seendee:saa
(money)	-onga	-o:ngaa
savoury	-nesipayisi	-nespaayee:see
to say ...	-sho	-sho
scarf (silk)	isikhafu	eeska:foo
	sikasilika	seegaaseeleekaa
(woollen)	isikhafu	eeska:foo
school	sikavolo	seegaavo:lo
scissors	isikele	eeske:le
Scotland	isiKotlandi	eeskotla:ndee
Scottish	isiKoshi	eesko:shee
scuba diving	i-scuba diving	eescuba diving
sculpture	umfanekiso oqoshiwe	oomfaanegee:so o!?oshee:we
sea	ulwandle	oolwaa:nɟe
seafood	ukudla kwasolwandle	oogoo:ɟaa kwaasolwaa:nɟe
to search	-cinga	-/?ee:ngaa
seasickness	-canuzeliswa ngulwandle	-/?aanooze-lee:swaa ngoolwaa:nɟe
seaside	ugu lolwandle	oogoo lolwaa:nɟe
at the seaside	ogwini	ogwee:nee
season (of year)	lolwandle	lolwaa:nɟe
seasonal	inkathi yonyaka	eenkaa:tee yonyaka
	-ngezinkathi zonyaka	-ngezeenkaa:tee zonyaa:gaa
	zonyaka	zonyaa:gaa
seat	isihlalo	ees4aa:lo
seatbelt	ibhande	eebaa:nde
	lokuphepha	logoope:paa
second	-esibili	-esbee:lee

English	Zulu	Pronunciation
second class	usekenikilasi	oosegene-keelaa:see
second (time)	isikhathi	eeskaa:tee
	sesibili	sesbee:lee
to see	-bona	-bo:naa
to sell	-thengisa	-tengee:saa
do you sell...?	uthengisa...?	ootengee:saa...?
sell-by date	usuku	ooso:goo
	ephelelwa	epele:lwaa
	ngalo	ngaa:lo
	isikhathi	eeskaa:tee
to send	-thuma	-too:maa
to pay	-khokha	-ko:kaa
separately	ngokwahlu-kanisa	ngogwaahloo-gaanee:saa
September	uSeptemba	oosepte:mbaa
serious	-bi kakhulu	-bee kaakoo:loo
to serve	-khonza	-ko:ndzaa
service (in restaurant, shop, etc.)	isevisi	eesevee:see

English	Zulu	Pronunciation
is service included?	ingabe nesevisi	eengaa:be
	ihlanganisiwe?	nesevee:see
		eet+aanggaanee-see:we?
service station	igalaji	eegaalaa:jee
set menu	imenu	eemenu
several	-mbalwa	-mbaa:lwaa
sex (gender)	ubulili	ooboolee:lee
(sexual intercourse)	ucansi	oo/?aa:ntsee
shade	umthunzi	oomtoo:ndzee
in the shade	emthunzini	emtoondzee:nee
to shake (bottle, etc.)	-nyakazisa	-nyaagaazee:saa
shampoo	ishampu	eeshaa:mpoo
to share	-abelana	-abelaa:naa
sharp (razor, knife)	-bukhali	-bookaa:lee
to shave	-shefa	-she:faa
shaver	umshini	oomshee:nee
	wokushefa	wogooshe:faa

English	Zulu	Pronunciation
she	u-	oo-
sheet (for bed)	ishidi	eeshee:dee
shirt	ihembe	eehe:mbe
shoe	isicathulo	ees/?aatoo:lo
shop	isitolo	eesto:lo
to shop	-thenga	-te:ngaa
shop assistant	umsizi	oomsee:zee
	wasesitolo	waasesto:lo
shopping	uxhaxha	oo//haa://haa
centre	lwezitolo	lwezeeto:lo
shore	ugu	oo:goo
short	-fushane	-fooshaa:ne
shorts	isikhindi	eeskee:ndee
shoulder	ihlombe	ee4o:mbe
to shout	-klabalasa	-klaabaalaa:saa
show	ukwenziwa	oogwendzee:waa
to show	-khombisa	-kombe:saa
shower (wash)	ishawa	eeshaa:waa
to have/take a shower	-ngena	-nge:naa
	eshaweni	eshaawe:nee
shower gel	i-gel	eegel
shut (closed)	yokushawa	yogooshaa:waa
sick (ill)	-valiwe	-vaalee:we
I feel sick	-gula	-goo:laa
	angizizwa	aangeeze:zwaa
	kahle	kaa:de
side	icala	ee/?aa:laa
sightseeing	uhambo	oohaa:mbo
tour	lokubukabuka	logooboo-gaaboo:gaa
sign (notice)	uphawu	oopaa:woo
to sign	-sayina	-saayee:naa
signature	isignisha	eeseegnee:shaa
silk	usilika	ooseelee:kaa
silver	isiliva	eeseelee:vaa
similar (to)	*	
since	kusukela	koosooge:laa
to sing	-cula	-/?oo:laa
single (unmarried)	*	

English	Zulu	Pronunciation
(bed)	umbhede	oombe:de
(room)	oyisingili	oyeeseengee:lee
	ikamelo	eekaame:lo
	eliyisingili	eleeyeesee-ngee:lee
single ticket	isingili	eeseengee:lee
sir (when addressing)	Mnumzane	mnoomzaa:ne
sister	udade	oodaa:de
sister-in-law	umlamu	oomlaa:moo
to sit	-hlala	-4aa:laa
sit down (command)	hlala phansi	4aa:laa paa:ntsee
size (clothes, shoe)	usayizi	oosaayee:zee
skin	isikhumba	eeskoo:mbaa
skirt	isiketi	eeske:tee
sky	isibhakabhaka	eesbaagaabaagaa
to sleep	-lala	-laa:laa
to sleep in	-lala isikhathi eside ekuseni	-laalaa eeskaatee ese:de egoose:nee
sleeping bag	isikhwama sokulala	eeskwaa:maa sogoolaa:laa
sleeping pill	iphilisi lokulala	eepeelee:see logoolaa:laa
slice (bread, salami, etc.)	ucezu	oo/'e:zoo
slide (photograph)	isilayidi	eeslaayee:dee
to slip	-shelela	-shele:laa
slow	kancane	kanj/aa:ne
to slow down	-ehlisa ijubane	-etee:saa eejoobaa:nee
slowly	ngokungasheshi	ngogoongaa-she:shee
small	-ncane	-ŋ/aa:ne
smell	iphunga	eepoo:ngaa
a bad smell	iphunga elibi	eepoo:ngaa elee:bee

smile	ukumamatheka	oogoomaa-maate:gaa	someone	umuntu othile	oomoo:ntoo otee:le
to smile	-mamatheka	-maamaate:gaa	something	okuthile	ogootee:le
smoke	intuthu	eentoo:too	sometimes	ngesinye isikhathi	ngesee:nye eeska:thi
to smoke	-bhema	-be:maa	son	indodana	eendodaa:naa
I don't smoke	angibhemi	aangeebe:mee	son-in-law	umkhwenyana	oomkwenyaa:naa
can I smoke?	ngingabhema?	ngeengaabe:maa?	song	iculo	ee//oo:lo
smoked	-fusiwe	-foosee:we	soon	ngokushesha	ngoogooshe:shaa
smooth	-shelela	-shele:laa	as soon as possible	ngangokuno-kwenzeka	ngogooshe:shaa ngaangogoono-gwendze:gaa
snack	isinekhi	eesne:kee	sore	-buhlungu	-booHoo:ngoo
snow	iqhwa	ee:!hwaa	to have a sore throat	-phethwe	-pe:twe ngoo-
soap	insipho	eentsee:po	sorry:	ngumphimbo	mpee:mbo
sober: to be sober	*		I'm sorry	ngiyaxolisa	ngeeyaa://o-lee:saa
socks	amasokisi	aamaasogee:see	soup	isobho	eeso:bo
sofa	usofa	ooso:faa	sour	-muncu	-moo:ɲ/oo
soft	-thambile	-taambee:le	south	iningizimu	eeneengee-zee:moo
soft drinks	iziphuzo	eezeepoo:zo			
some	ezingadaki	eezengaadaagee			
	*				

English	Zulu	
souvenir	isikhumbuzo	eeskoomboo:zo
space (room)	indawo	eendaa:wo
sparkling (wine)	iwayini elizoyizayo	eewaayee:nee eleezoyeezaa:yo
(water)	amanzi azoyizayo	aamaa:ndzee azoyeezaa:yo
to speak	-khuluma	-kooloo:maa
do you speak English?	ukhuluma isiNgisi?	ookooloo:maa eeseengee:see?
speciality	ikhethelo	eekethe:lo
speeding	ukweqa ijubane	oogwe:l?aa eejoobaa.ne
speed limit	ijubane elibekiwe	eejoobaa.ne eleebegee:we
to spell: *how is it spelt?*	lipelwa kanjani?	leepe:lwaa kaanjaa:nee?
to spend (money)	-chitha imali	-/hee:taa eemaa.lee
(time)	-chitha isikhathi	-/hee:taa eeskaa:tee
spice	isipayisi	eespaavee:see

English	Zulu	
spicy	-nesipayisi	-nespaayee:see
spider	isicabucabu	ees/?aaboo-/?aa:boo
to spill	-chitha	-/hee:taa
spirits (alcohol)	ugologo	oogolo:lo
spoon	isipuni	eespoo:nee
sport	umdlalo	oomtaa:lo
sports shop	isitolo semidlalo	eesto:lo semeetgaa:lo
spot (pimple)	induna	eendoo:naa
spring (season)	intwasahlobo	eentwaasaa+o:bo
(metal)	isipilingi	eespeelee:ngee
square (in town)	igceke	ee:g?e:ge
to squeeze	-nkamfula	-nkaamfoo:laa
stadium	inkundla yemidlalo	eenkoo:ntgaa yemeetgaa:lo
staff	abasebenzi	aabaasebe:ndzee
stain	ibala	eebaa:laa
stairs	isitebhisi	eestebe:see
stamp (postage)	isitembu	eeste:mboo
to stand (get up)	-sukuma	-soogoo:maa

English – Zulu

English – Zulu

English	Zulu	Pronunciation
(be standing)	-mi	-mee
star	inkanyezi	eenkaanye:zee
to start	-qala	-ʔaa:laa
starter (in meal)	izibiliboco zokuqala	eezeebeeleebo:/ʔo zogooʔaa:laa
station	isiteshi	eeste:shee
stay	ukuvakashela	oogoovaa-gaashe:laa
enjoy your stay (remain)	ukujabulele	oogoojaaboolele
to stay	-sala	-saa:laa
(reside for while)	-hlala	-ɬaa:laa
I'm staying at...	ngihlala e...	ngeeɬaa:laa e...
steak	isiteki	eeste:kee
to steal	-ntshontsha	-ncho:nchaa
step (stair)	isitebhisi	eestebee:see
stepfather	ubaba omusha	oobaa:baa omoo:shaa
stepmother	umama omusha	oomaa:maa omoo:shaa
stepson	indodana yokutholwa	eendodaa:naa yogooto:lwaa

English	Zulu	Pronunciation
stereo	isteriyo	eesteree:yo
still: still water	amanzi azolile	aamaa:ndzee aazolee:le
still (yet)	*	
sting	-tinyela	-teenye:laa
stolen	-ntshontshiwe	-nchonchee:we
stomach	isisu	eese:soo
to have a stomach ache	-phethwe yisisu	-pe:twe yeesee:soo
to stop	-ma	-maa
(stop doing)	-yeka	-ye:gaa
store (shop)	isitolo	eesto:lo
storey	isitezi	eeste:zee
storm	isiphepho	eespe:po
story	indaba	eendaa:baa
straightaway	ngokushesha	ngogooshe:shaa
straight on	-qonde ngqo	-ʔo:nde n̩go
strange	*	
straw	utshumo	oochoo:mo
(for drinking)	lokuphuza	logoopoo:zaa
strawberries	amasitrobheri	aamaastrobe:ree

English	Zulu	Pronunciation
street	isitaladi	eestaalaa:dee
street map	ibalazwe lezitaladi	eebaalaa:zwe lezeetaalaa:dee
strength	amandla	aamaa:nɟaa
stress	ukucindezeleka	oogoo/?ee-ndezele:gaa
strike (of workers)	isiteleka	eestele:gaa
stroke (haemorrhage)	ukuthwebuleka komzimba	oogootweboo-le:gaa komzee:mbaa
strong	-namandla	-naamaa:nɟaa
stuck	-bhajiwe	-baajee:we
student	isitshudeni	eeschoode:nee
student discount	isaphulelo sezitshudeni	eesaapoole:lo sezeechoode:nee
stuffed	-hlohliwe	-ɬoɬee:we
stung	-tinyelwe	-teenye:lwe
stupid	-nobuthutha	-nobootoo:taa
suddenly	ngokuzuma	ngogoozoo:maa
suede	iswede	eeswe:de
sugar	ushukela	ooshooge:laa
sugar-free	-ngenashukela	-ngenaa-shooge:laa
to suggest	-sikisela	-seegeese:laa
suit (man's)	isudi	eesoo:dee
suit (woman's)	isudi lowesifazane	eesoo:dee lowesfaazaa:ne
suitcase	isutikesi	eesooteeke:see
sum	ingqikithi	eenjlgeegee:tee
summer	ihlobo	eehlo:bo
summit	isiqongo	ees?o:ngo
sun	ilanga	eelaa:ngaa
to sunbathe	-lala elangeni	-laa:laa elaange:nee
sunburn	ukushiswa yilanga	oogooshee:swaa yeelaa:ngaa
Sunday	iSonto	eeso:nto
sunglasses	izibuko zelanga	eezeeboo:go zelaa:nga
sunny: it's sunny	libalele	leebaale:le
sunrise	ukuphuma kwelanga	oogoopoo:maa kwelaa:nga

English - Zulu

English – Zulu

English	Zulu	
sunscreen (lotion)	ukhilimu wokuvimba ilanga	ookeelee:moo wogoovee:mbaa eelaa:ngaa
sunset	ukushona kwelanga	oogoosho:naa kwelaa:ngaa
sunshade	isambulela selanga	eesaamboole:laa selaa:ngaa
sunstroke	ukuguliswa yilanga	oogoogoolee:swaa yeelaa:ngaa
suntan	ukubhashulwa yilanga	oogoobaa-shoo:lwaa yeelaa:ngaa
supermarket	isuphamakhethe	eesoopamaakete
supper (dinner)	isidlo	eesee:tjo
supplement	sakusihlwa	saagoosee:‡waa
to supply	iseleko	eesele:go
surname	-nika	-nee:gaa
surprise	isibongo	eesbo:ngo
to survive	isimangaliso	eesmaangaalee:so
to swallow	-sinda	-see:ndaa
	-gwinya	-gwee:nyaa

English	Zulu	
to sweat	juluka	-jooloo:gaa
sweater	iswetha	eeswe:taa
sweet	-mnandi	-mnaa:ndee
sweetener	isinandisi	eesnaandee:see
sweets	amaswidi	aamaaswe:dee
to swell (bump, eye, etc.)	-vuvuka	-voovoo:gaa
to swim	-bhukuda	-boogoo:daa
swimming pool	idamu lokubhukuda	eedaamoo logoo-boogoo:daa
swimsuit	izingubo zokubhukuda	eezeengoo:bo zogoobooboo-goo:daa
to switch off	-cima	-/?ee:maa
to switch on	-vula	-voo:laa
swollen	-vuvukele	-voovooge:le

T

English	Zulu	
table	itafula	eetaafoo:laa
table tennis	ithenisi letafula	eetenee:see letaafo:laa

English	Zulu		
table wine	iwayini lokuvula inhliziyo	eewaayee:nee logoovoo:laa een+eezee:yo	
tablet	iphilisi	-taa:taa	
to take	-thatha	-soo:saa	
to take away	-susa	-haa:mbaa	
to take off	-hamba		
to talk (to)	*		
tall	-de	-de	
tart	ikhekhe	eeke:ke	
taste	lephestrii	lepe:stree	
	ukunambitheka	oogoonaa-mbeete:gaa	
to taste	-nambitha	-naambee:taa	
can I taste it/ some?	ngingaku-nambitha?	ngeengaagoo-naambee:taa?	
tax	intela	eente:laa	
taxi	itekisi	eetegee:see	
tea	itiye	eetee:ye	
herbal tea	itiye lamakhambi	eetee:ye laamaakaa:mbee	

to teach	-fundisa	-foondee:saa
teacher	uthisha	ootee:shaa
team	iqembu	ee!'e:mboo
tear (in material)	ukudabula	oogoodaaboo:laa
	intsha	ee:nchaa
teenager	itshitshi	eechee:chee
(girl)	ibhungu	eeboo:ngoo
(boy)	amazinyo	aamaazee:nyo
teeth	ucingo	oo/'ee:ngo
telephone	isigxobo	ees/'go:bo
telephone box	socingo	so/'ee:ngo
telephone call	-shaya ucingo	-shaa:yaa oo/'ee:ngo
telephone card	ikhadi	eekaa:dee
	lokushaya	logooshaa:yaa
	ucingo	oo/'ee:ngo
telephone number	inombolo	eenombo:lo
	yocingo	yo/'ee:ngo
to telephone	-shaya ucingo	-shaa:yaa oo/'ee:ngo

English – Zulu

English	Zulu	Pronunciation
television	i-TV	eetv
to tell	-tshela	-che:laa
temperature	izinga lokushisa	eezee:ngaa logooshee:saa
to have a temperature	-phethwe yinfiva	-pe:twe yee-mfee:vaa
temporary	-esikhashana	-eskaashaa:naa
tennis	ithenisi	eetenee:see
tent	ithende	eete:nde
tent peg	ikhwengco lethende	eekwe:ŋ/go lete:nde
to test (try out)	-hlola	-4o:laa
to text	-thuma i-SMS	-too:maa eesms
than	kuna-	koo:naa-
to thank	-bonga	-bo:ngaa
thank you (singular)	ngiyabonga	ngeeyaabo:ngaa
thank you (plural)	siyabonga	seeyaabo:ngaa
thank you very much (singular)	ngiyabonga kakhulu	ngeyaabo:ngaa kaakoo:loo
(plural)	siyabonga kakhulu	seeyaabo:ngaa kaakoo:loo
that: that one	*	
the		
theatre	ithiyetha	etheeye:taa
theft	ukweba	oogwe:baa
their (people)	-bo	-bo
(animals)	-zo	-zo
them (people)	bona	bo:naa
(animals)	zona	zo:naa
there	laphaya	laapaa:yaa
there is/are...	*	
these (ones)	*	
they (people)	ba-	baa-
(animals)	zi-	zee-
thick (not thin)	-hlangene	-4aange:ne
thief	isela	eese:laa
thin (person)	-ondile	-ondee:le
thing	into	ee:nto
my things	izinto zami	eezeento zaa:mee
to think	-cabanga	-/?aabaa:ngaa

English	Zulu	Pronunciation
thirsty:		
I'm thirsty	ngomile	ngome:le
this/those	*	
throat	umphimbo	oompee:mbo
thumb	isithupha	eestoo:paa
thunderstorm	ukuqeqebula kwezulu	oogoo!?e!e-boo:laa kwe-zoo:loo
Thursday	uLwesine	oolwesee:ne
ticket	ithikithi	eeteegee:tee
a single ticket	isingili	eeseengee:lee
a return ticket	iritheni	eerete:nee
ticket office	ihhovisi elithengisa amathikithi	eehovee:see eleetengee:saa aamaateegee:tee
tide	ibuya	eeboo:yaa
high tide	amanzi aphakeme	aamaa:ndzee aapaage:me
low tide	ibuya elishile	eeboo:yaa eleeshee:le
tidy	-cociwe	-/o//?ee:we

English	Zulu	Pronunciation
to tidy up	-coca	-/o://?aa
tie	-bopha	-bo:paa
tight (fitting)	-mpintsha	-mpee:nchaa
tights	amathayithi	aamaataayee:tee
till (cash desk)	ikhisi lemali	eekee:see lemaa:lee
(until)	kuze kube ngo-	koo:ze koo:be ngo
till 2 o'clock	kuze kube ngo-2	koo:ze koo:be ngo2
time (of day)	isikhathi	eeskaa:tee
this time	ngalesi sikhathi	ngaale:see skaa:tee
what time is it?	yisikhathi sini?	yeeskaa:tee see:nee?
timetable	uhlelo lwezikhathi	oote:lo lwezeekaa:tee
tip (to waiter, etc.)	umbhanselo	oombaantse:lo
to tip (waiter, etc.)	-nika umbhanselo	-nee:gaa oombaantse:lo
tired	-khathele	-kaate:le

English – Zulu

English	Zulu			
to	*			
to London	elandani	elaandaa:nee		
to the airport	esikhumulweni	eskoomoo-lwe:nee se-		
	sezindiza	zeendee:zaa		
to Canada	ekhanada	ekana:daa		
toast (to eat)	ithosi	eeto:see		
tobacco	ugwayi	oogwaa:yee		
tobacconist's	othengisa	otengee:saa		
	ngogwayi	ngogwaa-yee		
today	namhlanje	naam-laa:nje		
together	kanyekanye	kaanyekaa:nye		
toilet	ithoyilethi	eetoyeele:tee		
toll (motorway)	umgwaqo	oomgwaa:i?o		
	onentela	onente:laa		
	utamatisi	ootaamaatee:see		
tomato	kusasa	koosa:saa		
tomorrow	kusasa	koosa:saa		
tomorrow morning	ekuseni	egoose:nee		
tomorrow afternoon	kusasa ntambama	koosa:saa ntaambaa:maa		

English	Zulu			
tomorrow evening	kusasa kusihlwa	koosaa:saa koosee:4waa		
tongue	ulimi	oolee:mee		
tonight	namhlanje ebusuku	naam4aa:nje eboosoo:goo		
too (also)	futhi	foo:tee		
it's too big	-khulu kakhulu	-koo:loo kaakoo:loo		
tools	amathuluzi	aamaatooloo:zee		
tooth	izinyo	eezee:nyo		
toothache	ubuhlungu bezinyo	ooboo4oo:ngoo bezee:nyo		
I have toothache	ngiphethwe yizinyo	ngeepe:twe yeezee:nyo		
toothbrush	ibhulashi lamazinyo	eeboolaa:shee laamaazee:nyo		
toothpaste	umuthi wokuxubha isitezi	oomoo:tee wogoo/?oo:baa eeste:zee esee-		
top: the top floor	esingaphezulu kakhulu	ngaapezoo:loo kaakoo:loo		

English	Zulu		English	Zulu
top (of pyjamas, bikini, etc.)	okwangenhla		toy	ithoyizi	eetoyee:zee
(of hill, mountain)	isiqongo		traditional	-komdabu	-komdaa:boo
on top of	*		traffic	izimoto	eezeemo:to
torch	ithoshi	eeto:shee	traffic jam	emgwaqweni	emgwaa!'we:nee
total (amount)	isamba	eesaa:mbaa	ukukhandana	oogookaandaanaa
to touch	-thinta	-tee:ntaa	traffic lights	kwezimoto	kwezeemo:to
tough (meat)	-lukhuni	-lookoo:nee	traffic warden	amarobhothi	aamaarobo:tee
tour	uhambo	oohaa:mbo	iphoyisa	eepoyee:saa
tourist	isihambi	eeshaa:mbee	trailer	lomgwaqo	lomgwaa:!'o
tourist (info)	ihhovisi	eehovee:see	inqodlana	eenjlobgaa:naa
office	lezihambi	lezeehaa:mbee		yemoto	yemo:to
towel	ithawula	eetaawoo:laa	train	isitimela	eesteeme:laa
tower	umbhoshongo	oombosho:ngo	by train	ngesitimela	ngesteeme:laa
town	idolobha	eedolo:baa	the first train	isitimela	eesteeme:laa
town centre	inkaba	eenkaa:baa		sokuqala	sokuqa:laa
	yedolobha	yedolo:baa	the last train	isitimela	eesteeme:laa
town hall	ihholo ledolobha	eeholo ledolo:baa		sokugcina	sogoo/gee:naa
town plan	ibalazwe	eebaala:zwe	the next train	isitimela	eesteeme:laa
	ledolobha	ledolo:baa	trainers/	esilandelayo	eseelaandelaayo
toxic	-noshevu	-noshe:voo	running shoes	amateki	aamaate:kee

English – Zulu

English	Zulu	pronunciation
tram	ithilamu	eeteelaa:moo
tranquillizer	umuthi	oomoo:tee
travel agent's	wokudambisa	wogoodaa-mbee:saa
to translate	-humusha	-hoomoo:shaa
to travel	-hamba	-haa:mbaa
travel agent's	ihhovisi	eehovee:see
	lezokuvakasha	lezogoo-vaagaa:shaa
tree	umuthi	oomoo:tee
trip	uhambo	oohaa:mboo
trolley	inqola	eenjlo:laa
trouble	inkathazo	eenkaataa:zo
trousers	ibhulukwe	eebooloo:gwe
true	-yiqiniso	-yee'eenee:so
to try	-zama	-zaa:maa
to try on	-linganisa	-leengaanee:saa
(clothes, shoes)		
t-shirt	isikibha	eeskee:baa
Tuesday	uLwesibili	oolwesbee:lee
to turn	-phendula	-pendoo:laa

to turn round	phenduka	pendoo:gaa
to turn off	-cima	-/'ee:maa
to turn on (light, etc.)	-vula	-voo:laa
to turn on (engine)	-dumisa	-doomee:saa
twice	kabili	kaabee:lee
twin-bedded room	ikamelo elinemibhede	eekaame:lo elinemeebe:de
twins	amawele	aamaawe:le
typical	-oqobo	-o'o:bo
tyre	ithaya	eetaa:yaa

U

ugly	-bi	-bee
umbrella (sunshade)	isambulela	eesaamboole:laa
uncle	umalume	oomaaloo:me
uncomfortable	-hlalisa kabi	-haalee:saa kaa:bee
unconscious	-ngezwa lutho	-nge:zwaa loo:to

English	Zulu	Pronunciation
under	*	
to understand	-qonda	-¹ʔo:ndaa
do you understand?	uyaqonda?	ooyaa¹ʔo:ndaa?
I don't understand	angiqondi	aangee¹ʔo:ndee
underwear	izingubo zangaphansi	eezeengoo:bo zaangaapaa:ntse
unemployed	*	
to unfasten (clothes, etc.)	-khumula	-koomoo:laa
United Kingdom	iBrithani	eebreetaa:nee
United States	iMelika	eemelee:kaa
university	iNyuvesi	eenyoove:see
unleaded petrol	i-unleaded	eeunleaded
unlikely	*	
to unpack (suitcase)	-khipha impahla	-kee:paa eempaa:ɬaa
unpleasant	*	
up: to get up (out of bed)	-vuka	-voo:gaa
upside down	-mapeketwane esitezi	-mapegetwaa:ne este:zee
upstairs	-phuthuma	-pootoo:maa
urgent	-si-	-see-
us	-sebenzisa	-sebendzee:saa
to use	-siza	-see:zaa
useful	-vamele	-vaame:le
usually	ngokuvamile	ngogoovaamee:le
U-turn	i-U-turn	eeuturn
V		
vacant	*	
vacation	iholide	eeholee:de
valid (ticket, driving licence, etc.)	-sebenzayo	-sebendzaa:yo
valley	isigodi	eesgo:dee
valuable	-yigugu	-yeegoo:goo
valuables	amagugu	aamaagoo:goo

English	Zulu	
value	inani	eenaa:nee
VAT	i-VAT	eevat
vegan	idelanyama	eedelaanyaa:maa
vegetables	imifino	eemeefee:no
vegetarian	izilanyama	eezeelaanyaa:maa
very	kakhulu	kaakoo:loo
view	indawo ebukwayo	eendaa:wo eboogwaa:yo
villa	indlu yesicebi	eendloo yesee:cebee
village	idolobhana	eedolobaa:naa
vineyard	isivini	eesvee:nee
virus	igciwane	eegcwaa:ne
visa	imvume yokungena ezweni	eemvoo:me yogoonge:naa ezwe:nee
visit	ukuhambela	oogoohaambe:laa
to visit	-vakasha	-vaagaa:shaa
visitor	isivakashi	eesvaagaa:shee
voice	izwi	ee:zwee
voicemail	imeyili lezwi	eemeyee:lee le:zwee
to vomit	-hlanza	-hlaa:ndzaa
voucher	ivawusha	eevaawoo:shaa

W

English	Zulu	
to wait for	-lindela	-leende:laa
waiter	uweta	oowe:taa
waiting room	ikamelo lokulinda	eekaame:lo logoolee:ndaa
to wake up	-vuka	-voo:gaa
Wales	i-Wales	eewales
walk	ukuhamba	oogoohaa:mbaa
to go for a walk	-hambahamba	-haambahaa:mbaa
to walk	-hamba ngezinyawo	-haa:mbaa ngezeenyaa:wo
wall	ubonda	oobo:ndaa
wallet	isikhwama semali	eeskwaa:maa semaa:lee
to want	-funa	-foo:naa
I want...	ngifuna...	ngeefoo:naa...
we want...	sifuna...	seefoo:naa...

English	Zulu		English	Zulu	
warm	-fudumele	eewaa:shee	watch	iwashi	eewaa:shee
it's warm (weather)	kufudumele	koofoodoome:le	to watch (look at)	-buka	-boo:gaa
it's too warm	kufudumele kakhulu	koofoodoome:le kaakoo:loo	water	amanzi	aamaa:ndzee
to warm up (milk, etc.)	-fudumeza	-foodoome:zaa	*drinking water*	amanzi okuphuza	aamaa:ndzee ogoopoo:zaa
to wash	-washa	-waa:shaa	*sparkling mineral water*	amanzi esiphethu azoyizayo	aamaa:ndzee espe:too aazoyeezaa:yo
to wash (oneself)	-geza	-ge:zaa	*still mineral water*	amanzi esiphethu avamile	aamaa:ndzee espe:too aavaamee:le
washing machine	umshini wokuwasha	oomshee:nee wogoowaa:shaa	water sports	imidlalo yasemanzini	eemeeʔgaa:lo yaa-semaandzee:nee
washing powder	insipho yokuwasha	eentsee:po yogoowaa:shaa	waves (on sea)	amagagasi	aamaagaagaa:see
washing-up liquid	insipho yokuwasha izitsha	eentsee:po yogoowaa:shaa eezee:chaa	way (manner)	umkhuba	oomkoo:baa
wasp sting	ukutinyelwa ngumuvi	oogooteenye:lwaa ngoomoo:vee	way (route)	indlela	eenʔje:laa
waste bin	umgqomo wezibi	oomʔgo:mo wezee:bee	way in (entrance)	umnyango	oomnyaa:ngo
			way out (exit)	indawo yokuphuma	eendaa:wo yogoopoo:maa
			we	si-	see-

weak	-buthakathaka
(coffee, etc.)	ikhofi
	elingamanzi
to wear	-gqoka
weather	izulu
weather forecast	isibikezelo
	sezulu
wedding	umshado
Wednesday	uLwesithathu
week	isonto
last week	ngesonto
	eledlule
next week	ngesonto
	elizayo
per week	ngesonto
this week	ngaleli sonto
weekend	impelasonto
weekly (per week)	masonto onke
to weigh	-linganisa
weight	isisindo

welcome (when addressing one person)	wamukelekile
well (healthy)	-phila
he's not well	akaphilile
I'm very well	ngiphila kahle
well done	kakhulu
(steak)	-vuthwe
Welsh	kakhulu
	iWelishi
west	intshonalanga
wet	-manzi
what?	-ni?
what is it?	yini?
wheelchair	isihlalo saba-
	khubazekile
when?	nini?
(at what time?)	ngasikhathi
	sini?
when is it?	-nini?

| waamoogele- |
| gee:le |
| -pee:laa |
| aagaapeelee:le |
| ngeepee:laa kaa:- |
| +e kaakoo:loo |
| -vootwe kaa- |
| koo:loo |
| eewelee:shee |
| eenchonaa- |
| laa:ngaa |
| -maa:ndzee |
| -nee? |
| yee:nee? |
| eeshaa:lo saabaa- |
| koobaazegee:le |
| nee:nee? |
| ngaaskaa:tee |
| see:nee? |
| -nee:nee? |

| -bootaagaa- |
| taa:gaa |
| eeko:fee elee- |
| ngaamaa:ndzee |
| -!go:gaa |
| eezoo:loo |
| eesbeegeze:lo |
| sezoo:loo |
| oomshaa:do |
| oolwestaa:too |
| eeso:nto |
| ngeso:nto |
| eletgoo:le |
| ngeso:nto |
| eleezaa:yo |
| ngeso:nto |
| ngaale:lee so:nto |
| eempelaaso:nto |
| maaso:nto o:nke |
| -leengaanee:saa |
| eeseesee:ndo |

English	Zulu	Pronunciation
where?	kuphi?	koo:pee?
where is it?	...kuphi?	...koo:pee?
where is the hotel?	ihhotela likuphi?	eehote:laa leegoo:pee?
which?	-phi?	-pee?
which (one/s)?	*	*
while	isikhathi	eeskaa:tee
in a while	emva kwesikhathi	e:mvaa kweskaa:tee
white	-mhlophe	-m+o:pe
who?	-ubani?	-oobaa:nee?
who is it?	ngubani?	ngoobaa:nee?
whole	-onke	-o:nke
wholemeal bread	isinkwa sikakolo	eesee:nkwaa seegaako:lo
whose: whose is it?	...kabani?	...gaabaa:nee?
why?	kungani?	koongaa:nee?
wide	-banzi	-baa:ndzee
width	ububanzi	ooboobaa:ndzee
wife	inkosikazi	eenkoseegaa:zee

English	Zulu	Pronunciation
to win	-wina	-wee:naa
wind	umoya	oomo:yaa
window (shop)	ifasitela	eefaaseete:laa
windscreen	ifasitela langaphambili	eefaaseete:laa laangaapaa-mbee:lee
windsurfing	ukugibela ipulangwe lokuntweza emanzini	oogoogeebe:laa eepoolaa:ngwe logoontwe:zaa emaandzee:nee
windy: it's windy	kunomoya	koonomo:yaa
wine	iwayini	eewaayee:nee
wine list	uhlu lwama-wayini	oo+oo lwamaa-waayee:nee
winter	ubusika	ooboose:gaa
with	*	*
with ice	-noayisi	-noaayee:see
with milk	-nobisi	-nobee:see
with sugar	-noshukela	-noshooge:laa
without	*	*

English – Zulu

English – Zulu

without ice	-ngena-ayisi	-ngenaa-ayee:see		
without milk	-ngenabisi	-ngenaabee:see		
without sugar	-ngenashukela	-ngenaashooge:laa		
woman	owesifazane	owesfaazaa:ne		
wonderful	-mangalisa	-maangaalee:saa		
wood	ukhuni	ookoo:nee		
wool	uvolo	oovo:lo		
word	igama	eegaa:maa		
work	umsebenzi	oomsebe:ndzee		
to work (person, car)	-sebenza	-sebe:ndzaa		
it doesn't work	*		wrong	*
world	izwe	ee:zwe	**X**	
worried	-khathazekile	-kaataazegee:le	X-ray	i-eksireyi	i-eksire:yee
worse	-bi kakhulu	-bee kaakoo:loo	to X-ray	-thatha	-taa:taa
to wrap (up)	-songa	-so:ngaa		i-eksireyi	ee-eksere:yee
to write	-bhala	-baa:laa	**Y**		
please write	ngicela	ngee/?e:laa	year	unyaka	oonyaa:gaa
it down	ukubhale	oogoobaa:le	last year	ngonyaka	ngonyaa:gaa
	phansi	paa:ntsee		odlule	otʒoo:le
			next year	ngonyaka	ngonyaa:gaa
				ozayo	ozaa:yo
			this year	ngalo nyaka	ngaa:lo nyaa:gaa
			yearly	njalo ngonyaka	njaa:lo
					ngonyaa:gaa
			yellow	-phuzi	-poo:zee
			yes	yebo	ye:bo
			yes please	ngingajabula	ngeengaa–
					jaaboo:laa
			yesterday	izolo	eezo:lo

yet: *not yet*	-ngakenzeki	-ngaagendze:gee
yoghurt	iyogathi	eeyogaa:tee
you	u-	oo-
young	-sha	-shaa
your	-kho	-ko
youth hostel	ihostela	eehoste:laa
	labasha	laabaa:shaa

Z

zero	iqanda	eel'aa:ndaa
zip	uziphu	oozee:poo
zone	isifunda	eesfoo:ndaa
zoo	izu	ee:zoo

Zulu – English

A

abantu	people	amagagasi	waves (on sea)
abantwana	children	amagilavu	gloves
abasebenzi	staff	amagugu	valuables
abazali	parents	ama-Ista	Easter
abazukulwane	grandchildren	ama-Ista	happy Easter!
-abelana	to share	amahle!	
-akha	to build	amajuweli	jewellery
akubhenywa	non-smoking (seat, compartment)	amalungiselelo	facilities
-ala	to refuse	amandla	strength
am	a.m.	anethonikhi	tonic water
amabhisikidi	biscuits	amanzi azolile	still water
amabhuthi	boots	amanzi	sparkling water
ama-contact lense	contact lenses	azoyizayo	
amadoda	men	amanzi esiphethu	mineral water
amafulethi	block of flats	amanzi	drinking water
amafutha	fat (noun), oil (for food)	okuphuza	
		amaphandle	countryside
		amaphoyisa	police (force)

amarobhothi	traffic lights
amashibusi	French fries, chips, crisps
amasiriyeli	cereal
amasokisi	socks
amasonto	fortnight
amabii	
amasutikesi akhe	his/her suitcases
amasutikesi ami	my suitcases
amaswidi	sweets
amateki	trainers, running shoes
amathayithi	tights
amathoyilethi abesifazane	ladies' (toilet)
amathoyilethi abesilisa	gents' (toilet)
amawele	twins
amazinyo	teeth

amehlo	eyes	
-amukela	to accept	
-anda	to increase	
-anele	enough	
-anga	to kiss	
ayikho inkinga	no problem	
-azi	to know (be aware of) (person, place)	

B

-ba	to become
-baba	bitter
-balulekile	important
-bamba	to catch
-bambekile	delayed
-banda	cold
-banzi	wide
-beka	to put (place)
-bhajiwe	stuck
-bhala	to write
-bhema	to smoke

-bhuka	to book, to reserve
-bhukela ngokweqile	to overbook
-bhukiwe	reserved
-bhukuda	to swim
-bhuleka	to brake
-bi kabi	awful
-bi kakhulu	serious, worse
-bika	to report (theft, etc.)
-bila	to boil
-bili	both
-bilisa	to boil (cause to boil)
-biza	to cost, to call
-biza imali eyeqileyo	to overcharge
-biza kakhulu	dear (expensive)
-boleka	to lend, to borrow

-bolile	off (rotten)
-bomvana	pink
-bomvu	red
-bona	to see, to realize
-bonga	to thank
-bopha	to tie, to fasten (seatbelt)
-buhlungu	painful, sore
-buka	to watch (look at), to look at
-bukeka	handsome
-bukhali	sharp (razor, knife)
-bulala	to kill
-buthakathaka	weak
-buya	to come back, to go back, to return (to a place)
-buyela	

Zulu – English

Zulu – English

-buyisa — to return (to return sth), to give back
-buyisela — to reimburse
-buyisela imali — to refund
-buza — to ask (a question)

C

-cabanga — to think
-canuzeliswa ngulwandle — seasickness
-cebile — rich (person)
-cela — please (request), to request
-cela indlela — to ask for directions
cha — no
cha, ngiyabonga — no thanks

-chaza — to describe, to explain
-chitha — to spill
-chitha imali — to spend (money)
-chitha isikhathi — to spend (time)
-cima — to switch off, to turn off (light, engine etc.)
-cinga — to search
-cishe — almost, about (approximately)
-cishile — off, out (light)
-coca — to tidy up
-cociwe — tidy
-cula — to sing
-cwathile — clear
-cwecwa — to peel (fruit)

D

-dabukile — sad

-dabuli — double
-dakiwe — drunk
-dala — old
-dalula — to declare
-dansa — to dance
-dayisa ezweni elingaphandle — to export
-de — tall, long
-dina — boring
-dinga — to need
-divosile — divorced
-dla — to eat
-dla ukudla kwakusihlwa — to have dinner
-dlala — to play (games)
-dlula — to overtake (in car)
-dlwengulwa — to be raped
-doba — to go fishing
-donsa — to pull

-dumisa	to turn on (engine)	emihla ngemihla	daily (each day)	**F**	
-dwa	alone	emini	at midday	-fa	to die
E		-enza	to do, to make	-fanayo	same
e-	in, to, at	-enza ibhizinisi	on business	-fanele uku-	to have to, must
ebusuku	at night	-enza ifothokhophi	to photocopy	-fika	to arrive, to come
edolobheni	in, into town	-enzeka	to happen	-fudumele	warm
eduze	close by	-enziwe ngezandla	hand-made	-fudumeza	to heat up, to warm up (milk, etc.)
-ehla	to go down, to get off (bus, etc.), to land	-eqa	to jump	-funa	to look for, to want
-ehlisa ijubane	to slow down	-esaba	to be afraid of	-funda	to read, to learn
eKhanada	in, to Canada	-esibili	second	-fundisa	to teach
ekhaya lakho	at your home	esitezi	upstairs (on the) first	-funeka	essential
ekhaya lami	at my home	esitezi sokuqala	floor	-fushane	short, low
ekhaya lethu	at our home	etafuleni	on the table	-fusiwe	smoked
ekuseni	in the morning	-ethula	to introduce	-futhi	too (also), again, and
eLandani	in, to London	-ezizwe ngezizwe	international		
-elula umzimba	to exercise				
-eluleka	to advise				

Zulu – English

Zulu – English

G

-gcina	last, to keep (retain)
-gcwalisa	to fill, to fill in (form)
-gcwele	full (e.g. hall)
-geza	to wash (oneself)
-geza izithombe	to develop (photos)
-gibela	to board (plane, train, etc.)
-gibela ibhayisikili	to cycle
-gibela ihhashi	to ride (horse)
-gibela isitimela esinye	to change trains
-gijima	to run
-gqoka	to wear, to dress
-gula	ill, sick

-guqubele	cloudy
-gwema	to avoid
-gwinya	to swallow

H

halala!	congratulations!
-hamba	to travel, to depart, to leave, to go, to take off
-hambahamba, hamba kahle	to go for a walk goodbye (to one person leaving)
-hamba ngezinyawo	to walk, to go on foot
-hlala	to live (in a place), to sit, to stay (reside for a while)
-hlalisa kabi	uncomfortable
-hlangana	to meet
-hlanganisiwe	included

-hlangene	thick (not thin)
-hlanza	to vomit, to clean
-hlanzekile	clean
-hlasela	to attack
-hle	beautiful, good, nice (person)
-hle kakhulu	great (wonderful), excellent
-hlehlisa	to postpone
-hleka	to laugh
-hlela	to organize, to arrange
-hlola	to test (try out), to check
-hlosa uku-	to intend to
-hlukile	different
-hola	to earn
-humusha	to translate

English	Zulu
account, bank	i-akhawunti
account, bill	i-alamu
alarm	
car alarm	i-alamu yemoto
allergy	i-aleji
ambulance	i-ambhulense
antihistamine	i-antihistamini
apple	i-apula
aspirin	i-aspirini
cash dispenser (ATM)	i-ATM
Australia	i-Australia
Ireland	i-Ayilendi
iron (for clothes, metal)	i-ayini
Irish	i-Ayirishi
stain	ibala
map, plan (map)	ibalazwe

Zulu	English
ibalazwe ledolobha	town plan
ibalazwe lemigwaqo	road map
ibalazwe lezitaladi	street map
ibele	breast
ibhabhalazi	hangover
ibhalbhu	bulb (light)
ibhamuza	blister
ibhande lokuphepha	seatbelt
ibhandeshi	dressing (for wound)
ibhange	bank
ibhangqa	pair
ibhanisi	bread roll
ibhanoyi	aeroplane, flight, plane (aircraft)
ibhantshi	jacket

Zulu	English
ibhantshi lemvula	waterproof jacket
ibhasi	bus, coach (bus)
ibhavulumu	bathroom
ibhayisikili	bicycle
ibhayisikobho	cinema
ibhega	burger, hamburger
ibhethri	battery
ibhishi	beach
ibhizinisi	business
ibhodlela	bottle
ibhodlela lamanzi	a bottle of water
ibhodlela lomntwana	baby's bottle
ibhokisi leposi	postbox
ibhotela	butter
ibhuku locingo	directory (telephone)
ibhulakufesi	breakfast

Zulu – English

Zulu – English

Zulu	English
ibhulashi lamazinyo	toothbrush
ibhulawuzi	blouse
ibhuloho	bridge
ibhulukwe	pants, trousers
ibhulukwe langaphansi	pants (underwear)
ibhungu	teenager (boy)
iBrithani	United Kingdom
ibuya	tide
ibuya elishile	low tide
icala	side
ichibi lemvelo	lake
iculo	song
idamu lokubhukuda	swimming pool
idayethi	diet
idelanyama	vegan
ideski	desk (furniture)
ideski lokuthola ukwaziswa	enquiry desk
idethi	date (social)
idola	dollar
idolo	knee
idolobha	city, town
idolobhana	village
i-draught lager	draught lager
iduku	handkerchief
i-eksireyi	X-ray
ifasitela	window
ifasitela langaphambili	windscreen
ifemu	company (firm)
ifilimu	film (movie, for camera)
ifomu	form (document)
ifosholo	spade
ifulethi	apartment, flat
igalaji	garage, petrol station, service station
igalari	gallery
igama	name, word
iganandoda	pear
igazi	blood
igceke	square (in town)
igciwane	virus
i-gel yokushawa	shower gel
igesi yokukhempa	camping gas
igilebhisi	grape
igremu	gram
ihembe	shirt
ihhashi	horse
iholo ledolobha	town hall
ihhotela	hotel
ihhovisi	office

Zulu	English
ihhovisi elithengisa amathikithi	ticket office
ihhovisi lezihambi	tourist (*info*) office
ihhovisi lezinto ezilahlekile	lost property office
ihhovisi lezokuvakasha	travel agent's
ihhovisi likakhonsela	consulate
ihhovisi lokubhuka	booking office
ihhovisi lokwamukela izihambi	reception (*desk*)
ihhovisi lomthwalo oshiyiwe	left-luggage (*office*)
ihlobo	summer
ihlombe	shoulder
iholide	vacation, holiday
iholide lomphakathi	public holiday
ihora	hour
ihora elilodwa	one hour
ihostela labasha	youth hostel
i-invoyisi	invoice
ijazi	coat
ijazi lemvula	raincoat
ijazi lokuntanta	life jacket
ijezi	pullover
ijubane elibekiwe	speed limit
ikalishi lengane	pushchair
ikamelo	room (*in house, hotel*)
ikamelo elinemibhede emibili	twin-bedded room
ikamelo eliyidabuli	double room
ikamelo eliyisingili	single room
ikamelo lami	my room
ikamelo lethu	our room
ikamelo lokulala	bedroom
ikamelo lokulinda	waiting room
ikati	cat
iketanga	chain
ikhabe	watermelon
ikhadi	card
ikhadi lebhizinisi	business card
ikhadi lesheke	cheque card
ikhadi lokugibela	boarding card

Zulu – English

Zulu – English

Zulu	English	Zulu	English	Zulu	English
ikhadi lokushaya ucingo	telephone card	ikhemisi	chemist's/pharmacy	ikhofi elingena-caffeine	decaffeinated coffee
ikhala	nose	ikhemisi elivulwe ebusuku	after-hours chemist	ikhofi elinobisi	white coffee
ikhamera	camera	ikhethelo	speciality	ikhofi elisheshayo	instant coffee
iKhanada	Canada	ikhilogremu	kilogram	ikhompathimenti	compartment
ikhanda	head	ikhilomitha	kilometre	ikhompuyutha	computer
ikhasi	page	ikhishi	kitchen	ikhona	corner
ikhasimende	client, customer	ikhishi lemali	cash desk/till	ikhondomu	condom
ikhawunta	counter (shop, bar, etc.)	ikhodi yeposi	postcode	ikhonsathi	concert
ikhawunta lokwaziswa	desk (information)	ikhodi yokushaya ucingo	dialling code	ikhophi	copy (duplicate)
ikhaya	home	ikhofi	coffee	ikhwalithi	quality
ikhefi	café	ikhofi elimnyama	black coffee	ikilasi	class
ikhekhe elikhulu	cake (large)	ikhofi elingamanzi	weak (coffee, etc.)	ikilogo	clock
ikhekhe elincane	cake (small)			ikusasa	future
ikheli	address			ikwata	quarter
ikheli [e-email	e-mail address			ikwindla	autumn
				i-lager	lager
				ilanga	sun

Zulu	English
ilantshi	lunch
ilawunji	lounge
ilayisense	licence
ilayisense yokushayela	driving licence
ilayitha	cigarette lighter
ilensi	lens (of camera, etc.)
ilifti	lift (elevator)
ilitha	litre
ilokwe	dress
ilondolo	dry-cleaner's
iloshini	cream (lotion)
imakethe	market
imali	money
imali eyiphepha	banknote
imali yokugibela	fare (bus, etc.),
imali yokungena	admission charge, entrance fee
imali yokuthela	rental
imamaledi	marmalade
imbali	flower
iMelika	America, United States
imenu	menu (card, set meal, set menu)
imeshi	match (sport)
imeyili lezwi	voicemail
imfiva	fever
imfiva ethimulisayo	hay fever
imfologo	fork (for eating)
imfuluwenza	flu
imfunda-makhwelo	beginner
imibhalo	documents
imibhede ehlangene	twin beds
imibuzo	inquiries
imidlalo yasemanzini	water sports
imifino	vegetables
imihla ngemihla	every day
imilimitha	millimetre
imini	midday
imininingwane	details
iminithi	minute
iminti	mint (herb)
imisa	mass (in church)
imisebenzi yezandla	crafts
imitha	metre, meter
imnyuziyemu	museum
imotho	motor
imoto	car
imoto eqashiwe	hired car

Zulu – English

Zulu – English

impahla	package	incwadi yamasheke	cheque book	indawo yokubalekela umlilo	fire escape (staircase)
impambano yemigwaqo	crossroads	incwadi yemithi kadokotela	prescription	indawo yokuhlala	accommodation
impela	quite (completely)			indawo yokuhlalisa abantu abahambayo	departure lounge
impelasonto	weekend	incwadi yeziqondiso	guidebook		
impendulo	answer	incwadi yokubhalisa	register		
impilo	health	incwajana	brochure	indawo yokukhempa	campsite
impumalanga	east	indaba	story	indawo yokudla nokudla kabili ngosuku	half board
impumputhe	blind (person)	indandatho	ring (on finger)		
imvula	rain	indawo	place, space (room)	indawo yokudla nokudla kukonke	full board
imvume	visa				
yokungena ezweni		indawo ebukwayo	view		
inani	rate (price), value	indawo yeholide	resort (holiday)		
inathi	nut (to eat)	indishi yesathelayithi	satellite dish		
incazelo	description				
incithakalo	ruins				
incwadi	letter, book				
incwadi	phrasebook				
yamabinzana					

Zulu	English	Zulu	English	Zulu	English
indawo yokupaka izimoto	car park	indlu yokudlela	dining room	ingqikithi	sum
indawo yokuphuma	way out (exit)	indlwanyana yokudayisela	kiosk (newsstand)	ingubo	blanket
indawo yokushaya ucingo	kiosk (phone box)	indoda	man	inhlanhla	luck
indawo yokuzalwa	place of birth	indodakazi	daughter	inhlanzi	fish
indlebe	ear	indodana	son	inhlawulo	fine (penalty)
indlela	directions, way (route)	indodana yokutholwa	stepson	inhlekelele	disaster
indlela yezinyawo	footpath	induna	spot (pimple)	inhliziyo	heart
indlela yokupheka	recipe	inethi likamiyane	mosquito net	inhlobo yegazi	blood group
indlu	house	ingadi	garden	inhlokodolobha	capital (city)
indlu yesicebi	villa	ingalo	arm	iningizimu	south
indlu yezivakashi	guesthouse	iNgilandi	England, Great Britain	inja	dog
		ingilazi	glass	injini	engine
		ingilazi yamanzi	a glass of water	inkaba yedolobha	city centre, town centre
		iNgisi	British	inkathi yonyaka	season (of year)
		ingozi	accident, danger	inkantini	bar
				inkanyezi	star
				inkathazo	trouble
				inkinga	problem
				inkohliso	fake

Zulu – English

Zulu – English

Zulu	English
inkokhelo	charge (fee), payment
inkomfa	conference
inkomishi	cup
inkonkoni	homosexual
inkosikazi	wife
inkukhu	chicken
inkumbulo	memory
inkundla	pitch (sport)
inkundla yemidlalo	stadium
inkungu	fog
inombolo	number (of room, house)
inombolo kamakhalekukhwini	mobile number
inombolo yocingo	phone number
inombolo yesikhahlamezi	fax number
inombolo yekamelo	room number
inomfi	gluten
i-Northern Ireland	Northern Ireland
inoveli	novel
inqola	carriage (railway), trolley
inqola yokudlela	restaurant car
inqola yomthwalo	luggage trolley
insika	pier
yamatshe	
insikazi	female (animal)
insingo	razor blades, razor
insipho	soap
insipho yokuwasha	washing powder
insipho yokuwasha	washing-up liquid
izitsha	
insizwa	fiancé
ethembise	
intombi	
intaba	mountain
intambo	line (telephone)
intandokazi	favourite
intela	tax, customs (duty)
into	thing
intokazi	lady
intombi	girl, girlfriend
intombi	fiancée
ethembise	
insizwa	
intongomane	peanut
intsha	teenagers

Zulu	English
intshonalanga	west
intunja	tunnel
intuthu	smoke
intwasahlobo	spring (season)
inxusa	embassy
inyakatho	north
inyama	flesh, meat
inyama eyosiwe	roast
inyama yengulube	pork
inyama yenyamazane	game (meat)
inyanga	month, moon
inyoni	bird
iNyuvesi	University
iNyuzilandi	New Zealand
i-oda	order (in restaurant)
ipaki	park
ipasi	pass (bus, train)
ipeni	pen
ipetshisi	peach
iphansi	bottom (of pool, etc.), floor
iphantshi	puncture
iphaseji	corridor
iphasela	parcel
iphasiphothi	passport
iphasiphothi yakhe	his/her passport
iphasiphothi yami	my passport
iphawundi	pound (weight)
iphepha	paper
iphephandaba	newspaper
iphilisi	tablet
iphilisi lokulala	sleeping pill
iphosikhadi	postcard
iphoyinti	quay
iphoyisa lomgwaqo	traffic warden
iphunga	smell
iphunga elibi	a bad smell
iphutha	fault (defect)
iposi	mail, post (letters); post office
ipulamu	plum
ipulatifomu	platform (railway)
ipulazi	farm
ipuleti	plate
iputumende	briefcase
iqanda	zero, egg
iqembu	team, party (political)
iqhugwane	hut (mountain)
iqhwa	snow
irakethi	racket
irayisi	rice
iritheni	return ticket
i-rosé	rosé wine
irozi	rose

Zulu – English

Zulu – English

isakhiwo	building	
isaladi	salad	
isamba	total (amount)	
isambulela	umbrella (sunshade)	
isambulela selanga	sunshade	
isandla	hand	
isango	gate	
isaphulelo	discount, reduction	
isaphulelo sezitshudeni	student discount	
isaziso	notice (warning), sign (notice)	
isela	thief	
iseleko	supplement	
isemeshi	sandwich	
isentimitha	centimetre	

isevisi	service (in restaurant, shop, etc.)
isevisi yokulethelwa ukudla ehhotela	room service
ishampeni	champagne
ishampu	shampoo
ishandu	bruise
ishawa	shower (wash)
isheke	cheque
ishidi	sheet (for bed)
isibalo	number (quantity)
isibani	light
isibhakabhaka	sky
isibhedlela	hospital
isibikezelo sezulu	weather forecast
isibitebile	rich (food)
isibonelelo	concession

isibongo	surname
isibulala magciwane	antiseptic
isibulalazi-nhlungu	painkiller
isicabucabu	spider
isicathulo	shoe
isicelo	request
isichazamazwi	dictionary
isicishamlilo	fire extinguisher
isidaki	alcohol
isidlo esikhulu	main course (of meal)
isidlo sakusihlwa	supper (dinner)
isifo	disease, illness
isifuba	chest (body)
isifuba somoya	asthma
isifunda	region, zone
isifundo	lesson
isigaba sokudla	course (of meal)

Zulu	English
isigcino	end
isignisha	signature
isigodi	valley, district
isigxobo socingo	payphone, telephone box
isihambi	tourist
isihlabathi	sand
isihlalo	chair, seat (chair)
isihlalo saba-khubazekile	wheelchair
isihlalo semoto somntwana	car seat (for child)
isihlambululi sisu	antacid
isihlobo	relation (family)
isihluthulela zonke	central locking
isikebhe	boat
isikebhe esigwedlayo	boat (rowing)
isikebhe esinenjini	motorboat
isikele	scissors
isiketi	skirt
isikhahlamezi	fax
isikhala sentaba	pass (mountain)
isikhalo	complaint
isikhathi	time (of day), while
isikhathi eside	for a long time
isikhathi sesibili	second (time)
isikhathi sokubonana	appointment
isikhiye semoto	car key
isikhindi	shorts
isikhumba	skin
isikhumbuzo	souvenir
isikhumulo sezindiza	airport
isikhungo	centre
isikhungo sokushintsha imali yakwamanye amazwe	bureau de change
isikhwama	bag, handbag, pocket
isikhwama semali	purse, wallet
isikhwama sokulala	sleeping bag
isikibha	t-shirt
isikole	school
isiKoshi	Scottish
isiKotilandi	Scotland
isikulufu sokuvula ibhodlela	bottle opener
isikweletu	credit (on mobile phone)

Zulu – English

Zulu - English

Zulu	English
isilayidi	slide (photograph)
isilibaziso	hobby
isiliva	silver
isilonda	cold sore
somkhuhlane	heartburn
isilungulelo	heartburn
isilwane	pet
esifuywayo	pet
isimangaliso	surprise
isimemo	invitation
isimiso soku-fudumeza	central heating
isimo	form (shape, style)
isimo esiphu-thumayo	emergency
isinambuzane	insect
isinandisi	sweetener
isinekhi	snack
isingili	single ticket
isiNgisi	English (language)
isinkwa	bread
isinkwa esisikiwe	sliced bread
isinkwa sikakolo	wholemeal bread
isipayisi	spice
isiphepho	storm
isipho	gift, present (gift)
isiphosiso	error, mistake
isiphuzo	drink
isipuni	spoon
isiqandisi	freezer
isiqhingi	island
isiqinisekiso	confirmation
isiqongo	summit, top (of hill, mountain)
isisefo	safe (for valuables)
isisindo	weight
isistisi	cystitis
isisu	stomach
isitabani	lesbian
isitaladi	street
isitebhisi	step (stair, stairs)
isiteki	steak
isiteleka	strike (of workers)
isitembu	stamp (postage)
isiteshi	station
isiteshi samabhasi	bus station
isiteshi samaphoyisa	police station
isiteshi sikaloliwe	railway station
isitezi	floor (storey)
isitezi esi-ngaphezulu kakhulu	the top floor
isithembiso	promise

Zulu	English
isithokelo	dressing (for food)
isithombe	photograph
isithupha	thumb
isithuthi sokuxhuma	connection (train, bus, etc.)
isithuthuthu	motorbike
isitimela	train
isitobhu samabhasi	bus stop
isitolo	shop, store
isitolo esine-minyango ehlukene	department store
isitolo semifino nezithelo	greengrocer's
isitolo sezincwadi	bookshop
isitolo sezingubo	clothes shop
isitolo sokudlela	restaurant
isitsha	jar (honey, jam, etc.)
isitshudeni	student
isivakashi	guest (house guest, in hotel), visitor
isivalanzalo	contraceptive
isivini	vineyard
isivumelwano	contract
isivuno	harvest (grape)
isixhawu sezimbali	bunch (of flowers)
isixuku	crowd, group, party (group)
isizwe	nationality
iso	eye
isobho	soup
isoka	boyfriend
isomisi zinwele	hairdryer
isonto	week, church
iSonto	Sunday
isoseji	sausage
isosi	sauce
istelingi	sterling
isteriyo	stereo
istifiketi	certificate
istifiketi somshuwalense	insurance certificate
isudi	suit (man's)
isudi lowesifazane	suit (woman's)
isupha-makhethe	supermarket
isutikesi	case (suitcase)
iswetha	sweater
itafula	table
itekisi	cab (taxi)
ithambo	bone
ithawula	towel
ithaya	tyre

Zulu – English

Zulu – English

Zulu	English
ithekethele	jellyfish
itheku	port (seaport)
ithende	tent
ithenisi	tennis
ithikithi	ticket
ithikithi lebhanoyi	air ticket
ithikithi lebhasi	bus ticket
ithilamu	tram
ithini	can
ithiyetha	theatre
ithoni yocingo	dialling tone
ithoshi	torch
ithoyilethi	toilet, lavatory
ithoyizi	toy
-ithu	our
itiye	tea
itiye	herbal tea
itshitshi	teenager (girl)

Zulu	English
ivavusha	voucher
i-Wales	Wales
iwashi	watch
iwashi elicushwayo	alarm clock
iwayini	wine
iwayini elizoyizaza	sparkling (wine)
iwayini lokuvula inhliziyo	house wine
iwayini lerestoranti	table wine
iWelishi	Welsh
iwolintshi	orange (fruit)
iyogathi	yoghurt
iyogathi enganongiwe	plain yoghurt
iYurophu	Europe
izambane	potato
izaphulelo	sales (reductions)

Zulu	English
izibi	rubbish
izibiliboco	hors d'oeuvre/
izibuko zokuqala	starter (in meal)
izibuko	glasses (spectacles)
izibuko zelanga	sunglasses
izidakamizwa	drug (narcotics)
izifakamwandle-beni	earphones
izikhungo ze-inthanethi	internet café
izikweletu	debts
izilanyama	vegetarian
izimonyo	cosmetics
izimoto emgwaqweni	traffic
izindaba	news (TV, radio, personal)
izindleko	cost, expenses

Zulu – English

izindwangu zomntwana	baby wipes
izinga lokushintshiselana	rate of exchange
izinga lokushisa	temperature
izingubo	clothes
izingubo zangaphansi	underwear
izingubo zokubhukuda	swimsuit, swimming costume
izinwele	chair
izinyane	lamb
izinyawo	feet
izinyo	tooth
izinyembezi zikalkhwini	liqueur
izipele zemoto	car parts, spare parts

iziphuzo ezingadaki	soft drinks
izithako	ingredients
izithelo	fruit
izolo	yesterday
izu	zoo
izulu	weather
izwe	country, world
izwi	voice

J

-jabula	happy, pleased
-jabulela	to enjoy
-jahile	in a hurry
-joyina	to join (become member)
-juluka	to sweat

K

-kabani?	whose?, whose is it?
kabili	twice
-kagesi	electric
kakhulu	very
kamuva	later
kancane	slow
kangakanani?	how much?
kaningi	often
kanjani?	how?
kanye	once
kanyekanye	together
-kazwelonke	national
-khala	to cry (weep)
-khanga	attractive
-khansela	to cancel
-khanya	on (light), to shine
-khathazekile	worried
-khathele	tired

Zulu – English

Zulu	English
-khe	his/her
-khesha isheke	to cash (cheque)
-khetha	to pick (choose), to prefer
-khipha impahla	to unpack (suitcase)
-khiya	to lock
-kho	your
-khohlwa	to forget
-khokha	to pay
-khokha ngokwahlukanisa	to pay separately
-khokhiwe	paid
-kholwa	to believe
-khombisa	to show
-khononda	to complain
-khonza	to serve
-khubazekile	handicapped
-khulelwe	pregnant
-khulu	big, great, large, main
-khuluma	to speak
-khumbula	to remember, to recognize
-khumula	to unfasten (clothes, etc.)
-khwehlela	to cough
-klabalasa	to shout
kodwa	but
-komdabu	traditional
konke	everything
-kopisha	to copy
-ku-	to, at, from; you
-kude	distant, far
kuhle!	(that's) good!
kulungile	all right (agreed), OK (agreed)
kuna-	than
-kungakephuzi	early
kungani?	Why?
kuphela	only
kuphi?	where?
...kuphi?	...where is it?
kusasa	tomorrow
kusasa ebusuku	tomorrow night
kusasa ekuseni	tomorrow morning
kusasa kusihlwa	tomorrow evening
kusasa ntambama	tomorrow afternoon
kuseduze?	is it near?
kusihlwa	evening, in the evening
kusukela	since
kuze kube ngo-	till (until)
kuze kube ngo-2	till 2 o'clock

-kwabantwana for children
-kwazi uku... to be able to
-kweleta to owe
-kwelinye izwe foreign
-kwemvelo natural

L

-lahlekelwa to lose
-lahlekelwe lost (object), missing (disappeared)
-lala to sleep
-lala elangeni to sunbathe
-lala isikhathi eside ekuseni to sleep in
lala kahle good night (singular)
-lala phansi to lie down
-lalela to listen to
-lambile to be hungry

-landa to collect (someone), to get (to fetch)
-landela to follow
-landelayo next (after)
lapha here
-letha to bring
libalele it's sunny
-limaza to damage, to hurt, to injure
-limele injured
-lindela to wait for
-linganisa to try on (clothes, shoes), to weigh
-lingene equal
-luhlaza blue, green
-lukhuni hard (not soft), tough (meat)
-lula light (not heavy), easy

-luma to bite (animal, insect), to itch
-lungele ready
-lungile fair (just)
-lungisa to mend, to fix (repair)
-lungiselela to plan, to prepare
-lunyiwe bitten (by animal, insect)
lutho nothing, none
lutho olunye nothing else
-lwa to fight

M

-ma to stop (come to a standstill)
mahhala free (costing nothing)
-mamatheka to smile
-mangalisa wonderful

Zulu – English

Zulu – English

Zulu	English
-mangalisayo	odd (strange)
manje	now
-manzi	wet
-mapeketwane	upside down
maphakathi	central
masinyane	fast, quickly
masinyane kakhulu	too fast
masonto onke	weekly (per week)
-matasa	busy, engaged (phone)
-mba eqolo	expensive
-mbalwa	few, several, a couple of...
-mema	to invite
-memezela	to announce
-mhlawumbe	perhaps
-mhlophe	white
-mi	my, to stand (be standing)
-minyene	crowded

Zulu	English
-minza	to drown
-mnandi	nice (enjoyable), pleasant, sweet
-mnandi kakhulu	delicious
-mngcingo	narrow
Mnumzane	sir (when addressing), Mr
-mnyama	black, dark
mpilonhle!	cheers! (before drinking)
-mpintsha	tight (fitting)
-mpofu	poor
-mpunga	grey
-muncu	sour

N

Zulu	English
-na-	to have
-nakekela	to look after
-nakuna-mbitheka	plain (unflavoured)

Zulu	English
-nalutho	empty
-namafutha	greasy
-namahlaya	funny (amusing)
-namandla	strong
-nambitha	to taste
namhlanje	today
namhlanje ebusuku	tonight
namhlanje kusihlwa	this evening
namhlanje ntambama	this afternoon
naphakade	forever
-ncane	little, a little, small
-ncanyana	less
-ncelisa	to breast-feed
-ncibilika	soluble
-nciphisa	to reduce
-ndiza	to fly
-nefenisha	furnished

Zulu	English
-nempilo	healthy
-nembile	right (correct)
-nengozi	dangerous
-nenhlanhla	lucky
-nesipayisi	spicy
-nesiyezi	dizzy
-nethezekile	comfortable
-nga...	can (to know how to)
-ngababi	mild (curry)
-ngakenzeki	mild (tobacco)
-ngakhokhe-lwa ntela	not yet
-ngaki?	duty-free
ngakweso-bunxele	how many?
ngakweso-kudla	left (on, to the left)
ngale nyanga	right (on, to the right)
ngaleli sonto	this month
	this week

Zulu	English
ngalesi sikhathi	this time
ngalo nyaka	this year
ngaphakathi	into, on the inside
ngaphansi kwesitezi	(on the) ground floor
ngaphezu kokuthathu	more than three
ngaphezulu	extra (more)
ngasese	private
ngasikhathi sini?	when? (at what time?)
-ngavamile	rare (uncommon)
-ngcolile	dirty
-ngcolisiwe	polluted
-ngcono	quite (rather)
ukwedlula konke	best
ngebhasi	by bus

Zulu	English
ngehora	per hour
ngeke	never
ngemoto	by car
ngempela	real
-ngena	to check in/come in/enter/get in (car)/go in
ngena!	come in!
-ngena eshaweni	to have/take a shower
-ngena-ayisi	without ice
-ngena-caffeine	decaffeinated
-ngenabisi	without milk
-ngenakwe-nzeka	impossible
-ngenashukela	sugar-free
-ngenasidaki	alcohol-free, non-alcoholic
-ngenisa	to admit

Zulu - English

Zulu – English

Zulu	English
-ngenisa izimpahla zakwelinye izwe	to import
ngenyanga edlule	last month
ngenyanga ezayo	next month
-ngenzeka	possible
ngeposi	by post, by mail
ngesikhahla-mezi	by fax
ngesikhathi	on time, during
ngesinye isikhathi	sometimes
ngesitimela	by train
ngesonto	per week
ngesonto eledlule	last week, a week ago
ngesonto elizayo	next week

Zulu	English
-ngezinkathi zonyaka	seasonal
-ngezwa lutho	unconscious
ngi-	I, I'm
ngi-	me
ngicela uphinde	pardon?
ngidinga...	I need...
ngifuna...	I want...
nginga...	I can, do you mind if I...?, do you mind?
ngingajabula	yes please
ngingatha nda...	I'd like...
ngisize!	help!
ngithanda...	I love...(food, activity, etc.)
ngithemba kanjalo	I hope so

Zulu	English
ngiya e...	I'm going to... (I will go to)
ngiyabonga (kakhulu)	thank you (very much) (singular)
ngiyaxolisa!	excuse me! (to get by), I'm sorry!
ngizo...	I'm going to... (I intend to)
ngoba	because
ngobusuku obudlule	last night
ngocingo	by phone
ngoFebruwari	February
ngokuka-kumelene	to belong to
ngokunga-sheshi	against
-ngokuno-kwenzeka	slowly
	probably

Zulu	English	Zulu	English	Zulu	English
ngokuphi-ndaphinda	frequent	ngonyaka ozayo	next year	nisale kahle	goodbye (to more than one person staying behind)
ngokushesha	immediately, quick, at once, soon, etc.	ngosuku	per day	njalo	always
ngangokuno-kwenzeka	as soon as possible	-ngqongqoza	to knock (on door)	njalo ngonyaka	yearly
ngokuvamile	usually	ngubani?	who is it?	-njani?	what kind?
ngokuzenza-kalelayo	automatic	-ngumJuda	Jewish	njenga-	like (preposition)
ngokuzuma	suddenly	-ni?	what	njengalokhu	like this
ngokwesi-bonelo	for example	nihambe kahle	goodbye (to more than one person leaving)	-nkamfula	to squeeze
ngoLwesihlanu	Friday	-nika	to give, to supply	-nke	whole, every, all
ngomkhumbi	by ship	-nika umbhanselo	to tip (waiter, etc.)	Nkosazana	Miss (when addressing), Ms (when addressing)
ngoMsombu-luko ozayo	next Monday	-ningi	a lot of, much, many	Nkosikazi	Mrs, Ms (when addressing)
ngonyaka odlule	last year	-ningi kakhulu	too much	-no-ayisi	with ice
		-nini?	when is it?	-nobisi	with milk
		nini?	when	-nobuthutha	stupid
		nilale kahle	good night (plural)	-nodaka	muddy

Zulu – English

Zulu – English

Zulu	English
-nokuphana	generous
noma	or, either … or
noma ikuphi	any
noma ngubani	anyone
noma yini	anything
-nomlando	historic
-nomsindo	loud
-nomuntu	engaged (toilet)
-nomusa	friendly, kind (person)
-nosawoti	salty
-noshevu	poisonous, toxic
-noshukela	with sugar
-nqatshelwe	prohibited, forbidden
-nqunta	to pluck
-nsundu	brown
ntambama	afternoon, in the afternoon
-ntshontsha	to steal
-ntshontshiwe	stolen
-nyakaza	to move
-nyakazisa	to shake (bottle, etc.)
-nyamalala	to disappear
-nye	another, more, other
-nzima	difficult, hard (not easy)
O	
-oda	to order (in restaurant)
ogwini lolwandle	at the seaside
okokuvula ukhokhi	corkscrew
okuncane kakhulu	minimum
-okuqala	first
okuseleyo	rest (remainder)
okuthile	something
okwamanje	at the moment
okwangenhla	top (of pyjamas, bikini, etc.)
olungisa izinwele	hairdresser
-omile	dry
-omisa	to blow-dry, to dry
-ondile	thin (person)
-onga	to save (money)
-opha	to bleed
-oqobo	typical
othengisa ngogwayi izwe	tobacconist's
owakwelinye izwe	foreigner
owaseYurophu	European
owesifazane	woman, female (human)
owesilisa	male (person)

Zulu – English

p		
-paka	to park	
-pakisha	to pack (luggage)	
phakathi	inside, middle	
phakathi endlini	indoors	
kwamabili	midnight, at midnight	
phakeme	high	
phambidlana	earlier	
phambili	forward, front	
phandle	outside	
phansi	low	
phansi esitezi	downstairs	
-phaphathekile	pale	
-phatha	to manage (to be in charge of)	
-phazamisa	to disturb	
-phefumula	to breathe	
-pheka	to cook (be cooking)	

-pheka ukudla	to cook a meal
-phelekezela	to accompany
-phelele	perfect
-phelelwe yisikhathi	to expire
-phenduka	to turn round
-phendula	to answer, to reply, to turn
-phephile	safe
-phesheya	abroad
-phethwe ngumphimbo	to have a sore throat
-phethwe yikhanda	to have a headache
-phethwe yimfiva	to have a temperature
-phethwe yisisu	to have a stomach ache
phezulu	top
-phi?	which?
-phila	well (healthy)

-phinda	to repeat
-pholile	cool, mild (weather, cheese)
-phothula	to complete
-phuka	fragile
-phukile	broken, broken down (car, etc.)
-phula	to break
-phuma	to go out (leave)
-phumula	to rest
-phuthuma	urgent
-phuza	to drink
-phuzi	yellow
-phuzile	late
pm	p.m.
-posa	to post

Q		
-qala	to begin, to start
-qandisiwe	frozen

Zulu – English

-qaphela	to be careful
qaphela!	be careful!
-qaqamba	to ache
-qasha	to hire
-qashisa	to hire out
-qeda	to finish
-qedile	finished
-qhubeka	to continue
-qinile	fit (medical)
-qinisa	to confirm
-qombola	to climb
-qonda	to understand
-qonde ngqo	straight on
-qondile	direct (train, etc.), flat (level)
-qotho	honest
-qukatha	to hold (contain)
-quleka	to faint

S

-sa-	still (yet)

-sala	to stay (remain)
sala kahle	goodbye (to one person staying behind)
san'bonani	good morning (plural), good day (plural), good afternoon (plural), good evening (plural)
-sawolintshi	orange (colour)
sawubona	good morning, good day, good afternoon, good evening (singular), hello (on telephone), hi!
-sayina	to sign
-se-	already, still (yet)

-sebenza	to work (person, machine, car), on (engine, etc.)
-sebenzayo	valid (ticket, driving licence, etc.)
-sebenzisa	to use
-seholideni	on holiday
-semfashinini	fashionable
-sesikhathini	period (menstruation)
-setshenziswa	free (not occupied)
-sha	new, fresh, young
-shadile	married
-shaya insimbi	to ring (bell)
-shaya ucingo	to telephone, to dial (a number)
-shayela	to drive

Zulu	English
-shayela ucingo	to ring sb
-shefa	to shave
-shelela	smooth, to slip
-sheshayo	express
-shibhile	cheap
-shintsha	to change, to exchange
-shintsha imali	to change money
-shintsha izingubo	to change clothes
-shisa	hot, to burn
-sho	to mean, to say
-shodile	flat (beer)
-shona	deep
-shonile	dead (humans)
-shiya	to leave behind
-si-	us
si-	we
sidinga...	we need...
sifuna...	we want...
-sika	to cut
-sikisela	to suggest
-sinda	to survive, heavy, to escape
-sindisa	to save (life)
-singa	we can
singathanda...	we'd like...
siyabonga (kakhulu)	thank you (very much) (plural)
-siza	to help, useful
-songa	to wrap (up)
-sukuma	to stand (get up)
-sunduza	to push
-susa	to take away, to remove
-swakeme	damp

T

Zulu	English
-tekula	to joke
-thakazelisa	exciting
-thakazelisayo	interesting
-thambile	soft
-thana	to pronounce
-thanda	to like, to love
-thandekayo	dear (in letter)
-thatha	to take
-thatha i-eksireyi	to X-ray
-thatha isithombe	to take a photograph
-thathe umhlalaphansi	retired
-themba	to hope
-thembisa	to promise
-thembisene umshado	engaged (to be married)
-thenga	to buy, to shop
-thengisa	to sell
-thinta	to touch
-thintana	to contact

Zulu	English
-thola	to discover, to find, to get (obtain)
-tholakala	available
-thosa	to fry
-thosiwe	fried, grilled
-thukuthele	angry
-thulile	calm, quiet (place)
-thuma	to send
-thumela i-e-mail	to e-mail
-thumela isikhahlamezi	to fax (document)
-thuma i-SMS	to text
-thumela umuntu isikhahlamezi	to fax (person)
-thuthukisa	to improve
-thwala	to carry
-tinyela	to sting
-tinyelwe	stung
-tshaja	to charge
-tshaja ucingo	to charge a phone
-tshela	to tell
-tshuza	to dive
-tusa	to recommend

U

Zulu	English
u-	he, she, you
u-Agasti	August
u-anyanisi	onion
u-ayisi	ice (cube)
u-ayisikhilimu	ice cream
ubaba	father
ubaba omusha	stepfather
ubabezala	father-in-law (father of husband)
ubani!?	who?
ubhavu	bath
ubhiya	beer
ubhontshisi	bean
ubisi	milk
ubisi lomntwana	baby milk (formula)
ubisi lukasoya	soya milk
ubisi olusha	fresh milk
ubisi oluyimpuphu	powdered milk
ubonda	wall
ububanzi	width
ubudala	age
ubude	length, height
ubugebengu	crime
ubuhlobo	relationship
ubuhlungu	pain
ubuhlungu bezinyo	toothache
ubulili	sex (gender)
ubuningi	quantity
ubusika	winter

Zulu	English
ubuso	face
ubusuku	night (night-time)
ubuthi obusekudleni	food poisoning
ubuntofontofo	luxury
ucansi	sex (sexual intercourse)
ucezu	slice (bread, salami, etc.), piece
ucingo	telephone
udade	sister
uDisemba	December
udizili	diesel
udokotela	doctor
udokotela wamazinyo	dentist
u-Ephreli	April
ufesikilasi	first class
ufulawa	flour
ugalikhi	garlic
ugesi	power (electricity)
ugologo	spirits (alcohol)
ugu	coast, shore
ugu lolwandle	seaside
ugwayi	tobacco
uhambo	journey, tour, trip
uhambo lokubukabuka	sightseeing tour
uhambo lwebhizinisi	business trip
uhambo oluhlanganisa izindleko zonke	package tour
uhambo oluqondiswayo	guided tour
uhele	row (theatre etc.)
uhhafu	half
uhhafu wehora	half an hour
uhhafu wemali yokugibela	half fare
uhhafu wentengo	half-price
uhlamvu lwemali	coin
uhlanga	race (people)
uhlelo lwezifundo	course (syllabus)
uhlelo lwezikhathi	timetable
uhlobo	kind (sort)
uhlu	list
uhlu lwamanani	price list
uhlu lwamawayini	wine list
ujanuwari	January
ujosaka	backpack

Zulu – English

Zulu – English

Zulu	English
uju	honey
ululayi	July
uluni	June
ujusi	juice
ujusi wama-wolintshi	orange juice
ujusi wezithelo	fruit juice
ukheshi	cash
ukhilimu	cream (food)
ukhilimu wokuvimba ilanga	sunscreen (lotion)
uKhisimusi	Christmas
uKhisimusi omuhle!	merry Christmas!
ukhokhi	cork
ukhokho	cocoa
ukhuluma isiNgisi?	do you speak English?
ukhuni	wood
ukubambezeleka	delay, hold-up (in traffic)
ukubhalisa	check-in (desk)
ukubhashulwa yilanga	suntan
ukubhuka	booking, reservation
ukudabula	tear (in material)
ukudla	food, meal
ukudla kwakusihla	dinner (evening meal)
ukudla kwasolwandle	seafood
ukudoba	fishing
ukufika	arrival
ukufudumeza	heating
ukuguliswa	refill
ukuguliswa yilanga	sunstroke
ukuhamba	walk, departure
ukuhambela	visit
ukuhlasela	attack (mugging, medical)
ukuhlaselwa yigciwane	infection
ukuhlolwa kwegazi	blood test
ukukhandana kwezimoto	traffic jam
ukukhansela	cancellation
ukulungisa	repair
ukulunywa	bite (animal)
ukulunywa yisilwane	bite (insect)
ukunambitheka yisinambuzane	taste, flavour (of ice cream, etc.)
ukungena	access
ukuntweza	sailing (sport)
ukuphambukiswa	diversion

Zulu	English
ukupholiswa nokufudunyezwa komoya	air-conditioning
ukuphumula	rest (relaxation)
ukuqasha	hire
ukuqasha imoto	car hire
ukuqeqebula kwezulu	thunderstorm
ukuqubuka	rash (skin)
ukuqumbelana	indigestion
ukusa	morning
ukushayisa	crash (car)
ukushiswa yilanga	sunburn
ukushona kwelanga	sunset
ukuthwebuleka komzimba	stroke (haemorrhage)

Zulu	English
ukutinyelwa ngumuvi	wasp sting
ukuvakashela	stay
ukuvaveka	fracture
ukuwa	fall
ukuwela	crossing (by sea)
ukuziphaqula	make-up
ukwabelana	exchange
ukwaziswa	information
ukweba	theft
ukweqa ijubane	speeding
ulamula	lemon
ulemoneti	lemonade
ulimi	language, tongue
uloliwe	railway
ulwandle	sea, ocean
ulwandle olunesivunguvungu	rough sea

Zulu	English
uLwesibili	Tuesday
uLwesine	Thursday
uLwesithathu	Wednesday
uma	if
uma kumnyama	after dark
umagazini	magazine
umajarini	margarine
umakalabha	crash helmet, helmet
umakhalekhukhwini	cellphone, mobile (phone)
umakoti	bride
umalokazana	daughter-in-law
umalume	uncle
umama	mother
umama omusha	stepmother
umamezala	mother-in-law (mother of husband)

Zulu – English

Zulu	English
uMashi	March
umasihlalisane	partner (cohabiting)
umaAustralia	Australian
umazisi	identity card
umbala	colour
umbambi zingcingo	receptionist
umbhangqwana	couple (two people)
umbhansela	tip (to waiter, etc.)
umbhede	bed
umbhede oyidabuli	double bed
umbhede oyisingili	single bed
umbhoshongo	tower
umbiko	report (of theft, etc.)
umbukiso	exhibition, performance (show)
umbuzo	question
umcimbi	celebration
umculo	music
umdanso	dance
umdlalo	play (at theatre), sport
umdwebo	picture (painting)
umentshishi	matches
uMeyi	May
umfana	boy
umfanekiso oqoshiwe	sculpture
umfowethu	brother
umfula	river
umfutho wegazi	blood pressure
umgede	cave
umgibeli	passenger
umgogodla wenhlanzi	bone (fish)
umgqekezi	burglar
uMgqibelo	Saturday
umgqomo wezibi	bin (dustbin), waste bin
umgudu	path
umgwaqo	road
umgwaqo omkhulu	motorway
umgwaqo onentela	toll (motorway)
umhalaliselo	congratulations
umhlane	back
umhlangano	meeting
umholi	guide (tourist guide)
umiyane	mosquito
umjaho	race (sport)
umKhanada	Canadian

Zulu	English	Zulu	English	Zulu	English
umkhiqizo wobisi	dairy produce	umlenze wengulube ophekiwe	ham (cooked)	nezimo eziphuthu-mayo	unit/A&E
umkhosi womlilo	fire alarm	umlilo	fire	umnyango wokuphulu-kundlela	emergency exit
umkhuba	way (manner)	umlindi	porter (for luggage)	umoya	wind
umkhuhlane	cold (illness), cough	umlingani	colleague, partner (business)	umphakathi	public
umkhuhlane wamaphaphu	bronchitis	umlomo	mouth	umphathi	manager
umkhulu	grandparent	uMmelikana	American	umpheki	chef
umkhwekazana	mother-in-law (mother of wife)	ummese	knife	umphimbo	throat
umkhwenyana	bridegroom, son-in-law	umndeni	family	umqamelo	pillow
umlamu	sister-in-law	umngane	friend	umqondo	idea
umlenze	leg	umntwana	baby, child	umsakazo	radio
umlenze wengulube ogqunyisiwe	ham (cured)	umnyango	door, entrance, way in	umsebenzi	job, work
		umnyango wabalimele	casualty department	umshado	wedding
		umnyango wezingozi	accident & emergency	umshanakazi	niece
				umshayeli	driver (of car)
				umshini	machine

Zulu – English

Zulu – English

Zulu	English
umshini wokuphendula ucingo	answerphone
umshini wokushefa	shaver
umshini wokuwasha	washing machine
umshuwalense	insurance
umshuwalense wemoto	car insurance
umsindo	noise
umsinga	current (air, water, etc.)
umsipha	muscle
umsizi wasesitolo	shop assistant
uMsombuluko	Monday
umthengisi	salesman/woman
umthunzi	shade
umthwalo	baggage, luggage
umthwalo wethu	our baggage
umugqa	line (mark), queue
umukhwe	father-in-law (father of wife)
umuntu	person
umuntu ngamunye	per person
umuntu ohola impesheni	pensioner
umuntu okhubazekile	disabled person
umuntu okhulile	adult
umuntu onesifo sikashukela	diabetic
umuntu othile	someone
umunwe	finger
umusa	favour
umuthi	drug (medicine), tree
umuthi obulala amagciwane	antibiotic
umuthi wokudambisa	tranquillizer
umuthi wokuhlambulula isisu	laxative
umuthi wokuhlanza	detergent
umuthi wokuxubha	toothpaste
umuthi womkhuhlane	cough mixture
umyalezo	message
umyeni	husband
umzala	cousin
umzanyana	babysitter
umzimba	body

Zulu	English
ungqoqwane	frost
uNovemba	November
unqengema	bank (river)
unyaka	year
uNyaka omusha	New Year
uNyaka omusha omuhle!	happy New Year!
unyawo	foot
u-Okthoba	October
upelepele	pepper (spice), chilli (fruit)
uphawu	sign (notice)
uphawu lomgwaqo	road sign
uphayi	pie (savoury)
uphepha	pepper (vegetable)
uphethelomu	fuel, petrol
uphizi	peas
uphuthini	dessert, pudding
upondo	pound (money)
usawoti	salt
usayizi	size (clothes, shoe)
usbari	brother-in-law
usekenikilasi	second class
uSepthemba	September
ushintshi	change (small coins)
ushokoledi	chocolate
ushokoledi ophuzwayo	drinking-chocolate
ushokoledi oshisayo	hot chocolate
ushukela	sugar
usikilidi	cigarette
usilika	silk
usizo loku-donswa kwemoto	breakdown van
usizo lokuqala	first aid
usofa	sofa
usomabhizinisi	businessman/woman
usuku	day, date (day of month or year)
usuku ephele-lwa ngalo isikhathi	sell-by date
usuku lokuzalwa	birthday, date of birth
utamatisi	tomato
uthando	love
uthisha	teacher
utshumo lokuphuza	straw (for drinking)
uvolo	wool
uweta	waiter
uwoyela	oil (for car)
uxhaxha lwezitolo	shopping centre

Zulu – English

Zulu – English

Zulu	English	Zulu	English	Zulu	English
uziphu	zip	-vula	to switch on, to open, to turn on (light, etc.) to unlock	ingavuzi igazi	to swell (bump, eye, etc.)
V		-vula isihluthulelo		-vuvuka	
-vakasha	to visit	-vuliwe	open	-vuvukele	swollen
-vala	to close	-vumela	to allow, to let (allow)	**W**	
-valelwe ngeqhwa	snowed in, up	-vumelana	to agree	-wa	to fall
-valiwe	closed (shop, etc.), shut (closed)	-vusa imizwa yothando	romantic	wamukelekile	welcome (when addressing one person)
-vamele	usual	-vuthiswe ngokweqile	overdone (food)	-washa	to wash
-vela e-	from	-vuthiwe	raw	-wela	to cross (road, sea, etc.)
-vikela ngomshuwalense	to insure	-vuthwe kakhulu	well done (steak)	-wina	to win
-vikelwe ngomshuwalense	insured	-vuthwe kancane	rare (steak)	**X**	
-vinjiwe	blocked	-vuthwe kancane kodwa	medium rare (meat)	-xabana	to quarrel
-vuka	to get up (out of bed), to wake up			-xega	loose (not fastened)
				-xhuma	to plug in
				-xuba	to mix

-ya	to leave (depart for), to go (somewhere)	-zalwa	born
		-zama	to try
-yakwazi uku-	to know how to do sth, can (to be able to)	-zayo	next (after)
		-zijabulisa	to have fun
		zonke izindawo	everywhere
-yakwazi ukubhukuda	to know how to swim	-zwa	to feel, to hear
yebo	yes		
-yeka	to stop (doing something)		
yena	him		
-yigugu	valuable		
-yimpoqo	compulsory		
-yindilingi	round		
yini?	what is it?		
-yiqiniso	true		
yisikhathi sini?	what time is it?		
-yisithulu	deaf		

Further titles in Collins' phrasebook range
Collins Gem Phrasebook

Also available as **Phrasebook CD Pack**
Other titles in the series

Afrikaans	Japanese	Russian
Arabic	Korean	Thai
Cantonese	Latin American	Turkish
Croatian	Spanish	Vietnamese
Czech	Mandarin	Xhosa
Dutch	Polish	Zulu
Italian	Portuguese	

Collins Phrasebook and Dictionary

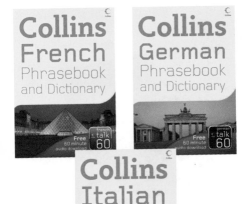

Other titles in the series

Greek Japanese Mandarin Polish Portuguese Spanish Turkish

Collins Easy: Photo Phrasebook

Also available as
**Phrasebook
CD Pack**

**Other titles
in the series**
Easy French
Easy Greek
Easy Italian

To order any of these titles, please telephone
0870 787 1732. For further information about all
Collins books, visit our website: www.collins.co.uk